ESSENTIAL POEMS
(TO FALL IN LOVE WITH)

ESSENTIAL POEMS
(TO FALL IN LOVE WITH)

EDITED BY

DAISY GOODWIN

HarperCollins*Publishers*

To All the *Essential Poems* Team

By arrangement with the BBC
BBC © BBC 1996
The BBC logo is a registered trademark of the
British Broadcasting Corporation and is used under licence.

HarperCollins*Publishers*
77–85 Fulham Palace Road,
Hammersmith, London w6 8jb

www.**fire**and**water**.com

Published by HarperCollins*Publishers* 2003
9 8 7 6 5 4 3 2

+(03

08980737

Full permissions information may be found on pp. 190–193

A catalogue record for this book
is available from the British Library

ISBN 0 00 716065 8

Set in PostScript Linotype Minion with Optima display
Typeset by Rowland Phototypesetting Ltd, Bury St Edmunds, Suffolk

Printed and bound in Great Britain by The Bath Press, Bath

CONTENTS

INTRODUCTION

As someone who has banged on about the therapeutic powers of poetry for years, I was delighted to find that there was more to my theory than personal conviction. A recent study by Robin Phillips of the Bristol Royal Infirmary observed 196 people with emotional problems and found that two-thirds of them felt better after reading or listening to poetry. What a satisfying thought: doctors pacifying their patients not with little blue pills that make the mouth go dry and the sex life shrivel, but with small doses of Browning and Keats. True, it takes a scintilla more concentration to read and understand a poem than it does to pierce a foil blister, but the effects are instantaneous, durable and for the most part benign. No one to my knowledge has claimed the undue influence of poetry as mitigating circumstances in a court of law.

Anyone who has had the good fortune to come across the right poem at the right moment will know what a shortcut it can be – it can fast forward your thoughts from chaos and confusion to conviction and clarity. About five years ago I was in a stomach twisting agony of indecision about my career: should I stay in the nice safe job where I knew everybody, or should I reinvent myself? In the end it wasn't my friends or mentors who helped me reach my decision but a poem by the Alexandrian writer C. P. Cavafy, called the 'The Big Decision'. There was one line that clinched it for me:

> Yet that no – the right no –
> Drags him down all his life.

It is a testament to the power of poetry that even in a slightly clunky translation, the right words in the right order can change your life. Sometimes you can find a poem too early – I first read Elizabeth Bishop's 'One Art' in my twenties, but I didn't have the taste buds then to appreciate its wry grandeur; now that I have become better acquainted with loss I wear its words of magnificent resignation as close to my heart as a bulletproof vest in a war zone.

> The art of losing isn't hard to master;
> So many things seem filled with the intent
> To be lost that their loss is no disaster.

Poems can even be prophylactic. Simply to have read Wendy Cope's 'Defining The Problem' has been my protection against some of the more virulent forms of romantic self-delusion:

> I can't forgive you. Even if I could,
> You wouldn't pardon me for seeing through you
> And yet I cannot cure myself of love
> For what I thought you were before I knew you.

So to call this book *Essential Poems* is not the contradiction it might first appear. Poems are not just beautiful things to be admired and revered but ultimately put away and forgotten. Good poetry *is* essential; it both deciphers our experience and chisels our reactions. Poems can make you laugh, cry, change your job, forgive others and even forgive yourself. They can also make you lose weight – I have no scientific evidence for this, but I know that when I am reading poems day and night for a book, I always lose ten pounds. Poetry is confectionery for the mind. It sounds far-fetched I know, but read the poems in the 'Hopelessly Devoted' section of this book and then try and eat a Kit Kat. It can't be done. Not if you're female, anyway.

Please don't read all the poems in this book at once. Poems, like chocolates, are there to be savoured. Gorge yourself and you will suffer from what is known as Stendhal Syndrome, where you become literally overpowered by great works of art. In order to avoid this condition, this book has been arranged in sections that follow the trajectory of love: from the restless beginnings of 'In the Mood for Love', through the erotic flights of 'Wild Nights' to the more sombre levels of 'End Games', 'Getting Over It' and 'Lost For Ever'. Whether you are single by choice or by circumstance, blissfully in love or unhappily married, I guarantee that there will be a poem here that will unlock something in your head like the last digit in a combination padlock. Find the right combination of words, and then, 'click' you're free. It may help to read the section heading first and only read on if the subject seems relevant to you right now. You may think this is rather poor value, but believe me, *all* the poems in this book will one day be relevant.

This book is designed to stand alone as a user's guide to love, but anyone who has seen the BBC2 series which accompanies it will know that all the poems collected here are as powerful in performance as they are on the page. I was by turns startled and abashed by the way they were interpreted on screen. These were poems that I thought I knew, indeed had chosen, and yet with each performance a new and unexpected layer of meaning was revealed. I was particularly struck by Damian Lewis's rendering of 'To His Coy Mistress' as an office Lothario. After all, seduction is the only solution to the everyday tedium of the office – Marvell's lines, 'the grave's a fine and private place/but none I think do there embrace,' could have been written for the many millions staring blankly at their computer screens at this very moment, wondering if they stand a chance with the new temp. Anna Massey's limpid reading of Emily Dickinson's 'After Great Pain a Formal Feeling Comes', was a chilling spin on a poem I had thought of as a hymn to acceptance. I suppose the ability of great poetry to transcend the ephemeral and the way it can be continually excavated for new seams of value gives it the edge over the pop song. There is a finite number of times that I can listen to Dylan's 'Shelter From the Storm' – much as I love it – but I could read Elizabeth Bishop's 'One Art' for ever and never be quite sure I had pinned it down for good.

This book could not have been put together without the inexhaustible energy and enthusiasm of the BBC2's show producer Alannah Richardson, the magisterial wisdom of its assistant producer Ned Williams, and the limitless imagination of the directors: James Harrison, Helen Simpson and Chloe Thomas. I must also thank the rest of the team – Adam Birley, Jane Donnelly, Kalita Corrigan, Katie Boston and Tori Nelson – for their extraordinary commitment to this extremely difficult project. I would also like to thank Jane Root for having the courage to commission it. Further thanks to Rashna Nekoo and Kristie Morris for their patience and support, to my editor Michael Fishwick for pretending I know what I'm talking about, Harry Thompson for the commas and semicolons, Connie Hallam for the clearances and my agent Derek Johns for enduring lengthy mobile phone calls. Finally, I am extremely grateful to my eldest daughter Ottie for letting me use her computer.

Meeting at Night

I

The grey sea and the long black land,
And the yellow half-moon large and low;
And the startled little waves that leap
In fiery ringlets from their sleep,
As I gain the cove with pushing prow,
And quench its speed i' the slushy sand.

II

Then a mile of warm sea-scented beach;
Three fields to cross till a farm appears;
A tap at the pane, the quick sharp scratch
And blue spurt of a lighted match,
And a voice less loud, thro' its joys and fears,
Than two hearts beating each to each!

Robert Browning

ESSENTIAL POEMS
(TO FALL IN LOVE WITH)

GETTING STARTED:
IN THE MOOD FOR LOVE

Romance – like the car keys, your birth certificate and an empty taxi – is never there when you need it. The conventional wisdom is to get out there and meet people, which is great for the organizers of car maintenance courses and salsa classes; but don't sign on the dotted line unless you are really fascinated by carburettors or enjoy close proximity to new varieties of aftershave. Far better to join a nunnery or sign up for a six-month stint on Mount Athos, where no woman has set foot in thousands of years, because the only guarantee is that when you do find love it will be when you least expect it.

Futility

It is silly –
This waiting for love
In a parlour,
When love is singing up and down the alley
Without a collar.

Helene Johnson

Where the Single Men Go in Summer

There is an island in a far-off sea,
Well hid, for to divulge its latitude were treason,
Whereto in swallow-flocks, and silently,
The single men migrate in summer season.
The millions of single men, having fled all year,
Come to this island utterly exhausted,
Murmur a brief thanksgiving on the pier,
Then breakfast on peanut butter and a chocolate
Frosted.
They tell male stories in the idioms of all nations,
Listen to ball games on the radio,
Hear minstrels celebrate the consummations
Of remarkable business deals. They never go
Away from this sanctuary till the season's sped.
In the summer hotels all over the world, the sad single girls
Wait in vain
For the One – personable, solvent, unwed –
Who might, but never does, arrive on the next train.

Nina Bourne

Green Velvet Suit

She was on the tube
I got on at Charing Cross
And like everyday
She didn't look at me
I even had a Green Velvet Suit
And a yellow bow tie
To make myself even more noticed
I dyed my hair really red

And I hope tomorrow
She will give me a glance
It's my very last chance
For the long week-end

Alvaro

Bloody Men

Bloody men are like bloody buses –
You wait for about a year –
And as soon as one approaches your stop
Two or three others appear.

You look at them flashing their indicators,
Offering you a ride.
You're trying to read the destinations,
You haven't much time to decide.

If you make a mistake, there is no turning back.
Jump off, and you'll stand there and gaze
While the cars and taxis and lorries go by
And the minutes, the hours, the days.

Wendy Cope

PLAYING THE DATING GAME

It would be so much easier if there were a foolproof recipe for making a relationship; take 400 grams of indifference, two unanswered phone calls, three nights when you're unavailable and a sprinkling of new underwear – and leave until set. You won't lose anything by following the advice laid out by Irish poet Frank O'Connor or poet A. S. J. Tessimond, but it is *male* advice. Margaret Atwood's words for would-be sirens are invaluable – Marilyn Monroe is a classic example of the 'Help me – only you can' woman. But sing your siren song with caution. It's not getting what you want, it's wanting what you get.

Two men in a dance hall

Tom laughs, is free and easy;
   And girls obey his call,
For whether they obey it
   He hardly cares at all.

But Edward burns with longing;
   And angry anxious pain
Cries from his eyes too loudly,
   Too eagerly, in vain.

A. S. J. Tessimond

Advice to Lovers

The way to get on with a girl
Is to drift like a man in a mist,
Happy enough to be caught,
Happy to be dismissed.

Glad to be out of her way,
Glad to rejoin her in bed,
Equally grieved or gay
To learn that she's living or dead.

Frank O'Connor

Siren Song

This is the one song everyone
would like to learn: the song
that is irresistible:

the song that forces men
to leap overboard in squadrons
even though they see the beached skulls

the song nobody knows
because anyone who has heard it
is dead, and the others can't remember.

Shall I tell you the secret
and if I do, will you get me
out of this bird suit?

I don't enjoy it here
squatting on this island
looking picturesque and mythical

with these two feathery maniacs,
I don't enjoy singing
this trio, fatal and valuable.

I will tell the secret to you,
to you, only to you.
Come closer. This song

is a cry for help: Help me!
Only you, only you can,
you are unique

At last. Alas
it is a boring song
but it works every time.

Margaret Atwood

HEALTH WARNING

Read these poems with attention if you are on the cusp of falling in love. As Robert Graves calls it, 'A bright stain on the vision/Blotting out reason', and Sheenagh Pugh, a 'judgement bypass'. But if you're on the edge it will take more than a poem, however fine, to stop you tumbling into the abyss.

Symptoms of Love

Love is a universal migraine,
A bright stain on the vision
Blotting out reason.

Symptoms of true love
Are leanness, jealousy,
Laggard dawns;

Are omens and nightmares –
Listening for a knock,
Waiting for a sign:

For a touch of her fingers
In a darkened room,
For a searching look.

Take courage, lover!
Could you endure such grief
At any hands but hers?

Robert Graves

It's Only Love

It's just this judgement bypass; nothing drastic.
(I'm told they do it without anaesthesia.)
It leaves your conscience supple as elastic.
One of the side-effects is mild amnesia:
facts get reshaped; pain slips your mind. Some blindness
is normal. Sufferers claim to see heaven
on earth; stars in dull eyes; wit in unkindness.
This commonly resists all treatment given.
It's not all bad. Granted, no flame-retardant
will work: but still, the toxins are a tonic.
The virus leaves you selfless, brave and ardent;
anyway, once you've got the thing, it's chronic.
Most people learn to live with the condition:
what kills them is the terror of remission.

Sheenagh Pugh

First Love

I ne'er was struck before that hour
   With love so sudden and so sweet,
Her face it bloomed like a sweet flower
   And stole my heart away complete.
My face turned pale as deadly pale
   My legs refused to walk away,
And when she looked, what could I ail?
   My life and all seemed turned to clay.

And then my blood rushed to my face
   And took my eyesight quite away,
The trees and bushes round the place
   Seemed midnight at noonday.
I could not see a single thing,
   Words from my eyes did start –
They spoke as chords do from the string,
   And blood burnt round my heart.

Are flowers the winter's choice?
   Is love's bed always snow?
She seemed to hear my silent voice,
   Not love's appeal to know.
I never saw so sweet a face
   As that I stood before.
My heart has left its dwelling-place
   And can return no more.

John Clare

HOPELESSLY DEVOTED

These poems really need no introduction. We've all been there, or will be there at some point. Although I suppose in the brave new world of non-smokers there may be those who don't realize quite how smitten Wendy Cope is when she says, 'I like you more than I would like/To have a cigarette'.

Celia, Celia

When I am sad and weary
When I think all hope has gone
When I walk along High Holborn
I think of you with nothing on.

Adrian Mitchell

Grey Room

Although you sit in a room that is grey,
Except for the silver
Of the straw-paper,
And pick
At your pale white gown;
Or lift one of the green beads
Of your necklace,
To let it fall;
Or gaze at your green fan
Printed with the red branches of a red willow;
Or, with one finger,
Move the leaf in the bowl –
The leaf that has fallen from the branches of the forsythia
Beside you . . .
What is all this?
I know how furiously your heart is beating.

Wallace Stevens

A Red, Red Rose

My Luve is like a red, red rose
   That's newly sprung in June:
My Luve's like the melodie
   That's sweetly played in tune.
As fair art thou, my bonnie lass,
   So deep in luve am I;
And I will luve thee still, my dear,
   Till a' the seas gang dry.

Till a' the seas gang dry, my dear,
   And the rocks melt wi' the sun!
I will luve thee still, my dear,
   While the sands o' life shall run.
And fare-thee-weel, my only Luve,
   And fare-thee-weel awhile!
And I will come again, my Luve,
   Tho' it were ten-thousand mile.

Robert Burns

Giving Up Smoking

There's not a Shakespeare sonnet
Or a Beethoven quartet
That's easier to like than you
Or harder to forget.

You think that sounds extravagant?
I haven't finished yet –
I like you more than I would like
To have a cigarette.

Wendy Cope

He wishes for the cloths of heaven

Had I the heavens' embroidered cloths,
Enwrought with golden and silver light,
The blue and the dim and the dark cloths
Of night and light and the half-light,
I would spread the cloths under your feet;
But I, being poor, have only my dreams;
I have spread my dreams under your feet;
Tread softly because you tread on my dreams.

W. B. Yeats

FINDING THE WORDS/
THE ONE THAT GOT AWAY

Everybody has a 'might have been' in their emotional treasury. A face on a train, a snatch of conversation at a party, the girl in the library; in my own case a man walking the other way on the Calle Lavallo in Buenos Aires twenty years ago. Shelley wrote 'Love's Philosophy' to Sophia Stacey, a young girl who had come to Italy with her chaperone to stay with him and his wife Mary Shelley. It is a persuasive poem but would he have written it if there had been no chaperone?

The 'ones that got away' are to be treasured; like irradiated strawberries, they never go off.

Love's Philosophy

The fountains mingle with the river
And the rivers with the ocean,
The winds of heaven mix for ever
With a sweet emotion;
Nothing in the world is single,
All things by a law divine
In one another's being mingle –
Why not I with thine?

See the mountains kiss high heaven,
And the waves clasp one another;
No sister-flower would be forgiven
If it distain'd its brother;
And the sunlight clasps the earth,
And the moonbeams kiss the sea –
What are all these kissings worth,
If thou kiss not me?

Percy Bysshe Shelley

The Look

Strephon kissed me in the spring,
    Robin in the fall,
But Colin only looked at me
    And never kissed at all.

Strephon's kiss was lost in jest,
    Robin's lost in play,
But the kiss in Colin's eyes
    Haunts me night and day.

Sara Teasdale

They Were in Love

They were in love, but neither
Would let the other know
And while they were dying of passion,
Hatred was all they'd show.

They parted at last, and only
In dream did their love live on.
Long ago they perished,
And scarcely knew they were gone.

Heinrich Heine

Momentous Words

What spiteful chance steals unawares
Wherever lovers come,
And trips the nimblest brain and scares
The bravest feelings dumb?

We had one minute at the gate,
Before the others came;
Tomorrow it would be too late,
And whose would be the blame!

I gazed at her, she glanced at me;
Alas! The time sped by:
'How warm it is today!' said she;
'It looks like rain,' said I.

Edward Rowland Sill

When I was fair and young

When I was fair and young, then favour graced me;
Of many was I sought their mistress for to be.
But I did scorn them all, and answered then therefore:
'Go! go! go: seek some other where, importune me no more!'

How many weeping eyes, I made to pine with woe!
How many sighing hearts! I have no skill to show.
Yet I the prouder grew, and still this spake therefore:
'Go! go! go: seek some other where, importune me no more!'

Then spake fair Venus' son, that proud victorious boy,
Saying: You dainty dame for that you be so coy?
I will pluck your plumes that you shall say no more:
'Go! go! go: seek some other where, importune me no more!'

As soon as he had said, such change grew in my breast,
That neither night nor day, I could take any rest.
Then lo! I did repent that I had said before:
'Go! go! go: seek some other where, importune me no more!'

Elizabeth I

WILD NIGHTS

Most novelists have real problems describing sex with any originality; poetry is a far more erotic medium. The intensity and rhythm of poetry have much more in common with the act than the most carefully tuned paragraph. Great poetry works intravenously. What other form would conjure up the tenderness of John Donne's lines from 'The Good Morrow':

> And now good morrow to our waking souls,
> Which watch not one another out of fear;
> For love, all love of other sights controls
> And makes one little room, an everywhere.

Wild Nights – Wild Nights!

Wild nights – Wild nights!
Were I with thee,
Wild nights should be
Our luxury!

Futile – the Winds –
To a Heart in port –
Done with the Compass –
Done with the Chart!

Rowing in Eden –
Ah, the Sea!
Might I but moor – Tonight
In Thee!

Emily Dickinson

To His Coy Mistress

Had we but world enough, and time,
This coyness, Lady, were no crime.
We would sit down and think which way
To walk and pass our long love's day.
Thou by the Indian Ganges' side
Shouldst rubies find: I by the tide
Of Humber would complain. I would
Love you ten years before the Flood,
And you should, if you please, refuse
Till the conversion of the Jews.
My vegetable love should grow
Vaster than empires, and more slow;
An hundred years should go to praise
Thine eyes and on thy forehead gaze;
Two hundred to adore each breast,
But thirty thousand to the rest;
An age at least to every part,
And the last age should show your heart.
For, Lady, you deserve this state,
Nor would I love at lower rate.

But at my back I always hear
Time's wingèd chariot hurrying near;
And yonder all before us lie
Deserts of vast eternity.
Thy beauty shall no more be found,
Nor, in thy marble vault, shall sound
My echoing song: then worms shall try
That long preserved virginity,

And your quaint honour turn to dust,
And into ashes all my lust:
The grave's a fine and private place,
But none, I think, do there embrace.
    Now therefore, while the youthful hue
Sits on thy skin like morning dew,
And while thy willing soul transpires
At every pore with instant fires,
Now let us sport us while we may,
And now, like amorous birds of prey,
Rather at once our time devour
Than languish in his slow-chapt power.
Let us roll all our strength and all
Our sweetness up into one ball,
And tear our pleasures with rough strife
Thorough the iron gates of life:
Thus, though we cannot make our sun
Stand still, yet we will make him run.

Andrew Marvell

The Cabala According to Thomas Alva Eddison

All objects give off sparks

Your tongue, for example, enters my mouth
& sends electricity along my veins

When we embrace in your office, your secretary turns blue
As the base of a flame

Your fly zips up & down making the sound
of a struck match

Even a struck match gives off sparks

My nails on the back of your knees
give off sparks
your nails on my thighs

Thighs, in general, give off sparks
But even the fuzz on thighs
gives off sparks

Sparks, in general, make the world go round
(There are, for example, spark plugs)

Plugs, in general, give off sparks

In & Out: the current of the world.

Erica Jong

The Good Morrow

I wonder by my troth, what thou and I
Did, till we lov'd? Were we not wean'd till then,
But suck'd on country pleasures, childishly?
Or snorted we in the seven sleepers' den?
T'was so; but this, all pleasures fancies be.
If ever any beauty I did see,
Which I desir'd, and got, t'was but a dream of thee.

And now good morrow to our waking souls,
Which watch not one another out of fear;
For love, all love of other sights controls,
And makes one little room, an everywhere.
Let sea-discoverers to new worlds have gone,
Let maps to other, worlds on worlds have shown,
Let us possess one world, each hath one, and is one.

My face in thine eye, thine in mine appears,
And true plain hearts do in the faces rest,
Where can we find two better hemispheres,
Without sharp north, without declining west?
Whatever dies, was not mix't equally;
If our two loves be one, or, thou and I
Love so alike, that none do slacken, none can die.

John Donne

THE MORNING AFTER

The morning after can be many things – warm and
glowing as in Hugo Williams's poem, or tortured with self-
reproach as in the Shakespeare sonnet that begins, 'The
expence of spirit in a waste of shame'. Whatever side of
the bed you've woken up on, you can be sure that some
poet has been there too.

Unfortunate Coincidence

By the time you swear you're his,
Shivering and sighing,
And he vows his passion is
Infinite, undying –
Lady, make a note of this:
One of you is lying.

Dorothy Parker

Saturday Morning

Everyone who made love the night before
Was walking around with flashing red lights
On top of their heads – a white-haired old gentleman,
A red-faced schoolboy, a pregnant woman
Who smiled at me from across the street
And gave a little secret shrug,
As if the flashing red light on her head
Was a small price to pay for what she knew.

Hugo Williams

Permissive Society

Wake, for the dawn has put the stars to flight,
And in my bed a stranger: so once more,
What seemed to be a good idea last night
Appears, this morning, sober, rather poor.

Connie Bensley

Sonnet 129

The expence of spirit in a waste of shame
Is lust, in action, and till action, lust
Is perjurd, murderous, bloody, full of blame,
Savage, extreame, rude, cruel, not to trust;
Enjoyd no sooner but despised straight;
Past reason hunted, and no sooner had,
Past reason hated, as a swallow'd bait
On purpose laid to make the taker mad:
Mad in pursut, and in possession so;
Had, having, and in quest to have, extreame,
A bliss in proof, and proved a very woe,
Before, a joy propos'd, behind, a dreame,
All this the world well knows; yet none knows well;
To shun the heaven that leads men to this hell.

William Shakespeare

TECHNICAL DIFFICULTIES

Has the medium altered the message? Does the course of true love run more smoothly now that we are instantly available? The ultimate intimacy, these days, is not seeing someone naked but catching a glimpse of their handwriting. The Maya Angelou poem is essential reading for anyone waiting for the phone to ring. Don't let it chaperone *your* life.

I w8 fr yr mesg the beep yr wrds of rude luv

I w8 fr yr mesg the beep yr wrds of rude luv
U mke me blush w
The curve of yr letters u tch me thru my palms, my eyes

Lucy Sweetman

The Telephone

It comes in black
and blue, indecisive
beige. In red and chaperones my life.
Sitting like a strict
and spinstered aunt
spiked between my needs
and need.

It tats the day, crocheting
other people's lives
in neat arrangements,
ignoring me,
busy with the hemming
of strangers' overlong affairs or
the darning of my
neighbours' worn-out
dreams.

From Monday, the morning of the week,
through mid-times
noon and Sunday's dying
light. It sits silent.
Its needle sound
does not transfix my ear
or draw my longing to
a close.

Ring. Damn you!

Maya Angelou

PASSING FANCIES

There is a lot to be said for the fling where, according
to Alice Walker, you feel 'warm, frisky,/moist-mouthed',
but most importantly 'could swim away/if forced to do
so'. The Canadian poet Earle Birney sums up this kind
of light romance:

> they winked when they met
> and laughed when they parted
> never took time
> to be brokenhearted.

If only it were that simple. If you can't reconcile yourself
to kissing the joy as it flies, then take comfort from
W. H. Auden's poem,

> . . . indifference is the least
> We have to dread from man or beast.

I'm Really Very Fond

I'm really very fond of you,
he said.

I don't like fond.
It sounds like something
you would tell a dog.

Give me love,
or nothing.

Throw your fond in a pond,
I said.

But what I felt for him
was also warm, frisky,
moist-mouthed,
eager,
and could swim away

if forced to do so.

Alice Walker

Never seek to tell thy love

Never seek to tell thy love,
Love that never told can be;
For the gentle wind does move
Silently, invisibly.

I told my love, I told my love,
I told her all my heart;
Trembling, cold, in ghastly fears,
Ah! she doth depart.

Soon as she was gone from me,
A traveller came by,
Silently, invisibly:
He took her with a sigh.

William Blake

From the Hazel Bough

He met a lady
    on a lazy street
hazel eyes
    and little plush feet

her legs swam by
    like lovely trout
eyes were trees
    where boys leant out

hands in the dark and
    a river side
round breasts rising
    with the finger's tide

she was plump as a finch
  and live as a salmon
gay as silk and
  proud as a Brahmin

they winked when they met
  and laughed when they parted
never took time
  to be brokenhearted

but no man sees
  where the trout lie now
or what leans out
  from the hazel bough

Earle Birney

Eternity

He who binds himself to a joy
Does the winged life destroy
But he who kisses the joy as it flies
Lives in Eternity's sunrise.

William Blake

The More Loving One

Looking up at the stars, I know quite well
That, for all they care, I can go to hell,
But on earth indifference is the least
We have to dread from man or beast.

How should we like it were stars to burn
With a passion for us we could not return?
If equal affection cannot be,
Let the more loving one be me.

Admirer as I think I am
Of stars that do not give a damn,
I cannot, now I see them, say
I missed one terribly all day.

Were all stars to disappear or die,
I should learn to look at an empty sky
And feel its total dark sublime,
Though this might take me a little time.

W. H. Auden

THE SOUL MATE

I like this poem by Maya Angelou, a woman who has now
written six volumes of autobiography. The idea of finding
the soul mate like a 'promised sunrise' is fabulously
seductive. Sadly Maya Angelou divorced her third husband,
the probable subject of this poem, after eight years of
marriage. Sometimes it is better to travel hopefully . . .

Where We Belong: A Duet

In every town and village,
In every city square,
In crowded places
I searched the faces
Hoping to find
Someone to care.

I read mysterious meanings
In the distant stars,
Then I went to schoolrooms
And poolrooms
And half-lighted cocktail bars.
Braving dangers,
Going with strangers,
I don't even remember their names.
I was quick and breezy
And always easy
Playing romantic games.

I wined and dined a thousand exotic Joans and Janes
In dusty dance halls, at debutante balls,
On lonely country lanes.
I fell in love forever,
Twice every year or so.
I wooed them sweetly, was theirs completely,
But they always let me go.
Saying bye now, no need to try now,
You don't have the proper charms.
Too sentimental and much too gentle
I don't tremble in your arms.

Then you rose into my life
Like a promised sunrise.
Brightening my days with the light in your eyes.
I've never been so strong,
Now I'm where I belong.

Maya Angelou

Love Poem

Sharing one umbrella
We have to hold each other
Round the waist to keep together.
You ask me why I'm smiling —
It's because I'm thinking
I want it to rain for ever.

Vicki Feaver

WHEN THE KISSING HAS TO STOP

You can have too much fun. Lord Byron wrote this poem as part of a letter to his friend Tom Moore after a particularly dissipated sojourn at the Venice festival. (Journalists in desperation sometimes call poetry the new rock 'n' roll, but judging the rate at which Byron lived, rock 'n' roll is the new poetry.) Byron writes in his letter, 'I find the sword wearing out the scabbard though I have just turned the corner of twenty-nine.'

Roger McGough's poem plays with the same sentiment but instead of the sword outwearing its sheath, he has ten milk bottles turning into cheese; not very rock 'n' roll!

So We'll Go No More A Roving

So we'll go no more a roving
　　So late into the night,
Though the heart be still as loving,
　　And the moon be still as bright.

For the sword outwears its sheath,
　　And the soul wears out its breast,
And the heart must pause to breathe,
　　And love itself have rest.

Though the night was made for loving,
　　And the day returns too soon,
Yet we'll go no more a roving
　　By the light of the moon.

Lord Byron

Ten Milk Bottles

ten milk bottles standing in the hall
ten milk bottles up against the wall
next door neighbour thinks we're dead
hasnt heard a sound he said
doesn't know we've been in bed
the ten whole days since we were wed

noone knows and noone sees
we lovers doing as we please
but people stop and point at these
ten milk bottles a-turning into cheese

ten milk bottles standing day and night
ten different thicknesses and
different shades of white
persistent carolsingers without a note to utter
silent carolsingers a-turning into butter

now she's run out of passion
and theres not much left in me
so maybe we'll get up
and make a cup of tea
then people can stop wondering
what they're waiting for
those ten milk bottles a-queuing at our door
those ten milk bottles a-queuing at our door

Roger McGough

HOW CAN I BE SURE?

We would all like to know for certain that we have found
the right person, that we have made the right emotional
investment. But remember there is no guaranteed rate of
return . . . You can do all the research you like, but in the
end, any proposal is a leap of faith.

Maybe

Maybe he believes me, maybe not.
Maybe I can marry him, maybe not.
Maybe the wind on the prairie,
The wind on the sea, maybe,
Somebody somewhere, maybe, can tell.
I will lay my head on his shoulder
And when he asks me I will say yes,
Maybe.

Carl Sandburg

Proposal

Let's fall in love –
In our mid-thirties
It's not only
Where the hurt is.

I won't get smashed up
Should you go
Away for weekends –
We both know

No two people
Can be completely
All-sufficient.
But twice weekly

We'll dine together
Split the bill,
Admire each other's
Wit. We will

Be splendid lovers,
Slow, well-trained,
Tactful, gracefully
Unrestrained.

You'll keep your flat
And I'll keep mine –
Our bank accounts
Shall not entwine.

We'll make the whole thing
Hard and bright.
We'll call it love –
We may be right.

Tom Vaughan

Alone

Each lover has a theory of his own
About the difference between the ache
Of being with his love, and being alone:

Why what, when dreaming, is dear flesh and bone
That really stirs the senses, when awake,
Appears a simulacrum of his own.

Narcissus disbelieves in the unknown;
He cannot join his image in the lake
So long as he assumes he is alone.

The child, the waterfall, the fire, the stone,
Are always up to mischief, though, and take
The universe for granted as their own.

The elderly, like Proust, are always prone
To think of love as a subjective fake;
The more they love, the more they feel alone.

Whatever view we hold, it must be shown
Why every lover has a wish to make
Some other kind of otherness his own:
Perhaps, in fact, we never are alone.

W. H. Auden

WONDER WEDLOCK

Glorious poems for the big day. The passage from *The Prophet*, which is fast becoming a wedding institution – 'Let there be spaces in your togetherness,/And let the winds of the heavens dance between you' – leaves more room for manoeuvre in volatile emotional markets than the magnificent finality of, 'What therefore God hath joined together, let no man put asunder'.

But if you want to pull out every organ stop then head for 'Marriage Morning' by Tennyson. They don't write them like that any more!

Marriage Morning

Light, so low upon earth,
You send a flash to the sun.
Here is the golden close of love,
All my wooing is done.
Oh, the woods and the meadows,
Woods where we hid from the wet,
Stiles where we stay'd to be kind,
Meadows in which we met!

Light, so low in the vale
You flash and lighten afar,
For this is the golden morning of love,
And you are his morning star.
Flash, I am coming, I come,
By meadow and stile and wood,
Oh, lighten into my eyes and heart,
Into my heart and blood!

Heart, are you great enough
For a love that never tires?
O heart, are you great enough for love?
I have heard of thorns and briers.
Over the thorns and briers,
Over the meadows and stiles,
Over the world to the end of it
Flash for a million miles.

Alfred Lord Tennyson

from *The Prophet*

You were born together, and together you
    shall be for evermore.
You shall be together when the white wings
    of death scatter your days.
Ay, you shall be together even in the silent memory
    of God.
But let there be spaces in your togetherness.
And let the winds of the heavens dance between you.

Love one another, but make not a bond of love:
Let it rather be a moving sea between the shores
    of your souls.
Fill each other's cup but drink not from one cup.
Give one another of your bread but eat not from
    the same loaf.
Sing and dance together and be joyous, but let each
    one of you be alone,
Even as the strings of a lute are alone though they
    quiver with the same music.

Give your hearts, but not into each other's keeping.
For only the hand of Life can contain your hearts.
And stand together yet not too near together:
For the pillars of the temple stand apart,
And the oak tree and the cypress grow not in each
    other's shadow.

Kahlil Gibran

At the Wedding March

God with honour hang your head.
Groom, and grace you, bride, your bed
With lissome scions, sweet scions
Out of hallowed bodies bred.

Each be other's comfort kind:
Déep, déeper than divined.
Divine charity, dear charity.
Fast you ever, fast bind.

Then let the march tread our ears:
I to him turn with tears
Who to wedlock, his wonder wedlock.
Déals triumph and immortal years.

Gerard Manley Hopkins

The Confirmation

Yes yours, my love, is the right human face.
I in my mind had waited for this long,
Seeing the false and searching for the true,
Then found you as a traveller finds a place
Of welcome suddenly amid the wrong
Valleys and rocks and twisting roads. But you,
What shall I call you? A fountain is a waste,
A well of water in a country dry,
Or anything that's honest and good, an eye
That makes the whole world bright. Your open heart,
Simple with giving, gives the primal deed,
The first good world, the blossom, the blowing seed,
The hearth, the steadfast land, the wandering sea,
Not beautiful and rare in every part.
But like yourself, as they were meant to be.

Edwin Muir

HAPPY TOGETHER

Sumptuous poems about the pleasures of intimacy. The Gloire de Dijon rose of Lawrence's title is one of the hardiest plants in existence. It was written for Frieda von Richthofen, who left her husband and three children for Lawrence. When this poem was published in a book called *Look! We have come through!*, Aldous Huxley commented that 'reading these poems was like opening the wrong bedroom door', and Bertrand Russell remarked that 'They may have come through, but I don't see why I should look'. Today, Lawrence's poems seem remarkably modern in their unflinching combination of sensuality and tenderness.

Gloire de Dijon

When she rises in the morning
I linger to watch her;
She spreads the bath-cloth underneath the window
And the sunbeams catch her
Glistening white on the shoulders,
While down her sides the mellow
Golden shadow glows as
She stoops to the sponge, and her swung breasts
Sway like full-blown yellow
Gloire de Dijon roses.

She drips herself with water, and her shoulders
Glisten as silver, they crumple up
Like wet and falling roses, and I listen
For the sluicing of their rain-dishevelled petals.
In the window full of sunlight
Concentrates her golden shadow
Fold on fold, until it glows as
Mellow as the glory roses.

D. H. Lawrence

It is Marvellous to Wake up Together

It is marvellous to wake up together
At the same minute; marvellous to hear
The rain begin suddenly all over the roof,
To feel the air clear
As if electricity has passed through it
From a black mesh of wires in the sky.
All over the roof the rain hisses,
And below, the light falling of kisses.

An electrical storm is coming or moving away;
It is the prickling air that wakes us up.
If lightning struck the house now, it would run
From the four blue china balls on top
Down the roof and down the rods all around us,
And we imagine dreamily
How the whole house caught in a bird-cage of lightning
Would be quite delightful rather than frightening;

And from the same simplified point of view
Of night and lying flat on one's back
All things might change quite easily,
Since always to warn us there must be these black
Electrical wires dangling. Without surprise
The world might change to something quite different,
As the air changes or the lightning comes without our blinking.
Change as our kisses change without our thinking.

Elizabeth Bishop

MARRIAGE BLOWS

If the poems in the previous section celebrate the delights
of togetherness, the poems that follow point out the pitfalls
of familiarity. I particularly like John Updike's poem, 'All
the While', about the ineffable strangeness of the
completely familiar:

> you stay as unaccountable
> as the underwear set to soak
> in the bowl where I brush my teeth

All the While

Upstairs to my downstairs
echo to my silence
you walk through my veins shopping
and spin food from my sleep

I hear your small noises
you hide in closets without handles
you surprise me from the cellar
your foot-soles bright black

You slip in and out of beauty
and imply that nothing is wrong
Who sent you?
What is your assignment?

Though years sneak by like children
you stay as unaccountable
as the underwear set to soak
in the bowl where I brush my teeth

John Updike

Dear Diary

Today my wife called me
   a 'pompous old fart.'
We were hugging at the time
   and did not spring apart,
though her words were deliberate
   and struck at my heart.

It's a fearsome business,
   This loving and being loved.
Would anyone try it
   if they hadn't been shoved
by a force beyond resistance –
   velvet-fisted and iron-gloved?

Christopher Reid

Hash Wednesday

last wednesday
  it all clicked

   you only wanted me for my loveandaffection
                              my generosity
                              and my undyingfaithfulness

(to you my prizegiven rosaries meant nothing,
my holy relics, merely relics)

Begone oh Belial's daughter
I wash my hands of you in holy water

next year i will live alone
and breed racehorses
in the attic

Roger McGough

Intimates

Don't you care for my love? she said bitterly.

I handed her the mirror, and said:
Please address these questions to the proper person!
Please make all requests to head-quarters!
In all matters of emotional importance
please approach the supreme authority direct!
So I handed her the mirror.

And she would have broken it over my head,
but she caught a sight of her own reflection
and that held her spell-bound for two seconds
while I fled.

D. H. Lawrence

A story wet as tears

Remember the princess who kissed the frog
so he became a prince? At first they danced
all weekend, toasted each other in the morning
with coffee, with champagne at night
and always with kisses. Perhaps it was
in bed after the first year had ground
around she noticed he had become cold
with her. She had to sleep
with a heating pad and down comforter.
His manner grew increasingly chilly
and damp when she entered a room.
He spent his time in water sports,
hydroponics, working on his insect
collection.
       Then in the third year
when she said to him one day, my dearest,
are you taking your vitamin pills daily,
you look quite green, he leaped
away from her.
       Finally on their
fifth anniversary she confronted him.
'My precious, don't you love me any
more?' He replied, 'Rivet. Rivet.'
Though courtship turns frogs into princes,
marriage turns them quietly back.

Marge Piercy

wearing the collar

I live with a lady and four cats
and some days we all get
along.

some days I have trouble with
one of the
cats.

other days I have trouble with
two of the
cats.

other days,
three.

some days I have trouble with
all four of the
cats.

and the
lady:

ten eyes looking at me
as if I was a dog.

Charles Bukowski

Home is the Hunter

She's watched for his return
at each day's evening, his briefcase
stuffed as if with deermeat,
umbrella a spent spear.
Forty years of triumphal entrances,
attentive welcomings, end in this
gift-loaded euphoric homecoming.
Something near to fear

stirs in her. The house
has been hers throughout the core
of every day, close shelter
for her busy morning hours,
her re-creative afternoons.
Now it opens its traitor door,
switches allegiance to his clamour,
his masterfulness, his more

insistent needs. How long had she
dug, hoed and planted the suburban
flower-patch, made it colourful
and fragrant for his weekend
leisure? Now he comes in with the air
of a pioneer, as if her patient garden
were wilderness for his first
cultivation; and she'll pretend

(habits are hard to break) when called on
to admire, that everything he grows
is magical, as if no million years
but he alone made this summer's rose.

Pamela Gillilan

TWO SCHOOLS OF THOUGHT

Two poems with disturbing revelations for either sex.
For women, Glyn Maxwell's poem proves that football *is*
all he really cares about. Men, on the other hand, should
take the message of Liz Lochhead's poem to heart: what
a woman says and what she actually means are not the
same thing *at all*.

The Perfect Match

There is nothing like the five minutes to go:
Your lads one up, your lads one down, or the whole
Thing even. How do you actually feel,
What you truly know,
Is that your lads are going to do it. So,

However many times in the past the fact
Is that they didn't, however you screamed and strained,
Pummelled the floor, looked up and groaned
As the Seiko ticked
On, when the ultimate ball is nodded or licked.

The man in the air is you. Your beautiful wife
May curl in the corner yawningly calm and true,
But something's going on with you
That lasts male life.
Love's one thing, but this is the Big Chief.

Glyn Maxwell

I Wouldn't Thank You for a Valentine

(rap)

I wouldn't thank you for a Valentine.
I won't wake up early wondering if the postman's been.
Should 10 red-padded satin hearts with sticky sickly saccharine
Sentiments in very vulgar verses I wouldn't wonder if you
    meant them.
Two dozen anonymous Interflora roses?
I'd not bother to swither over who sent them!
I wouldn't thank you for a Valentine.

Scrawl SWALK across the envelope
I'd just say 'Same Auld Story
I canny be bothered deciphering it –
I'm up to here with Amore!
The whole Valentine's Day Thing is trivial and commercial,
A cue for unleasing clichés and candyheart motifs to which
    I personally am not partial.'
Take more than singing Telegrams, or pints of Chanel Five,
    or sweets,
To get me ordering oysters or ironing my black satin sheets.
I wouldn't thank you for a Valentine.

If you sent me a solitaire and promises solemn,
Took out an ad in the Guardian Personal Column
Saying something very soppy such as 'Who Loyes Ya, Poo?
I'll tell you, I do, Fozzy Bear, that's who!'
You'd entirely fail to charm me, in fact I'd detest it
I wouldn't be eighteen again for anything, I'm glad I'm past it.
I wouldn't thank you for a Valentine.

If you sent me a single orchid, or a pair of Janet Reger's in a
    heartshaped box and declared your Love Eternal
I'd say I'd not be caught dead in them they were politically
    suspect and I'd rather something thermal.
If you hired a plane and blazed our love in a banner across the skies;
If you bought me something flimsy in a flatteringly wrong size;
If you sent me a postcard with three Xs and told me how you felt
I wouldn't thank you. I'd melt.

Liz Lochhead

PARENTHOOD

So far the poems in this book have been about the vagaries
of romantic love, but it seems appropriate after a slew of
words on marriage and settling down to include poems
about parenthood. The ones here could not be more
different and yet they all touch on the same paradox: every
parent wants to cocoon their child, in Sylvia Plath's phrase
'. . . fill it with colour and ducks/The zoo of the new', while
at the same time knowing that the other part of parenting is
making them independent. As C. Day-Lewis says so
poignantly:

> . . . selfhood begins with a walking away
> And love is proved in the letting go.

Child

Your clear eye is the one absolutely beautiful thing.
I want to fill it with colour and ducks,
The zoo of the new

Whose names you meditate –
April snowdrop, Indian pipe,
Little

Stalk without wrinkle,
Pool in which images
Should be grand and classical

Not this troublous
Wringing of hands, this dark
Ceiling without a star.

Sylvia Plath

Lullaby

Go to sleep, Mum
I won't stop breathing
suddenly in the night

Go to sleep, I won't
climb out of my cot and
tumble downstairs

Mum, I won't swallow
the pills the doctor gave you or
put hairpins in electric
sockets, just go to sleep

I won't cry
when you take me to school and leave me:
I'll be happy with other children
my own age.

Sleep, Mum, sleep.
I won't
fall in the pond, play with matches,
run under a lorry or even consider
sweets from strangers.

No, I won't
give you a lot of lip,
not like some.

I won't sniff glue,
Fail all my exams,
Get myself/
My girlfriend pregnant.
I'll work hard and get a steady/
really worthwhile job.
I promise, go to sleep.

I'll never forget
to drop in/phone/write
and if
I need any milk, I'll yell

Rosemary Norman

Walking Away

For Sean

It is eighteen years ago, almost to the day –
A sunny day with the leaves just turning,
The touch-lines new-ruled – since I watched you play
Your first game of football, then, like a satellite
Wrenched from its orbit, go drifting away

Behind a scatter of boys. I can see
You walking away from me towards the school
With the pathos of a half-fledged thing set free
Into a wilderness, the gait of one
Who finds no path where the path should be.

That hesitant figure, eddying away
Like a winged seed loosened from its parent stem,
Has something I never quite grasp to convey
About nature's give-and-take – the small, the scorching
Ordeals which fire one's irresolute clay.

I have had worse partings, but none that so
Gnaws at my mind still. Perhaps it is roughly
Saying what God alone could perfectly show –
How selfhood begins with a walking away,
And love is proved in the letting go.

C. Day-Lewis

THE GRASS IS GREENER

A recent analysis of DNA samples belonging to people with the same surnames showed that one in six children were the result of 'paternal misdirection'.* If that figure is extrapolated over the entire population and adjusted to include illicit unions that have no offspring, it is not only Tory politicians who can resist anything but temptation. None of these poems makes very comforting reading for the unfaithful. Infidelity clearly isn't a good idea, but then at least one in six of us knows that already . . .

* 'Paternal misdirection' if mum was playing away

The Fired Pot

In our town, people live in rows.
The only irregular thing in a street is the steeple;
And where that points to God only knows,
And not the poor disciplined people!

And I have watched the women grow old,
Passionate about pins, and pence, and soap,
Till the heart within my wedded breast grew cold,
And I lost hope.

But a young soldier came to our town,
He spoke his mind most candidly.
He asked me quickly to lie down,
And that was very good for me.

For though I gave him no embrace –
Remembering my duty –
He altered the expression of my face,
And gave me back my beauty.

Anna Wickham

may i feel said he

may i feel said he
(i'll squeal said she
just once said he)
it's fun said she

(may i touch said he
how much said she
a lot said he)
why not said she

(let's go said he
not too far said she
what's too far said he
where you are said she)

may i stay said he
(which way said she
like this said he
if you kiss said she

may i move said he
is it love said she)
if you're willing said he
(but you're killing said she

but it's life said he
but your wife said she
now said he)
ow said she

(tiptop said he
don't stop said she
oh no said he)
go slow said she

(cccome?said he
ummm said she)
you're divine!said he
(you are Mine said she)

E. E. Cummings

Story of a Hotel Room

Thinking we are safe – insanity!
We went in to make love. All the same
Idiots to trust the little hotel bedroom.
Then in the gloom . . .
. . . And who does not know that pair of shutters
With the awkward hook on them
All screeching whispers? Very well then, in the gloom
We set about acquiring one another
Urgently! But on a temporary basis
Only as guests-just guests of one another's senses.

But idiots to feel so safe you hold back nothing
Because the bed of cold, electric linen
Happens to be illicit . . .
To make love as well as that is ruinous.
Londoner, Parisian, someone should have warned us
That without permanent intentions
You have absolutely no protection
If the act is clean, authentic, sumptuous,
The concurring deep love of the heart
Follows the naked work, profoundly moved by it.

Rosemary Tonks

Infidelities

After he'd gone,
she found money in the sheets,
fallen when he pulled his trousers off.
Gathering the coins into a small pile
she set them on the window ledge.
They sat, gathering dust, guilt,
until one day her husband
scooped them into his pocket.
Small change for a call
he couldn't make from the house.

Moyra Donaldson

Taken in Adultery

Shadowed by shades and spied upon by glass
Their search for privacy conducts them here,
With an irony that neither notices,
To a public house; the wrong time of the year
For outdoor games; where, over gin and tonic,
Best bitter and potato crisps, they talk
Without much zest, almost laconic,
Flipping an occasional remark.
Would you guess that they were lovers, this dull pair?
The answer, I suppose, is yes, you would.
Despite her spectacles and faded hair
And his worn look of being someone's Dad
You know that they are having an affair
And neither finds it doing them much good.
Presumably, in one another's eyes,
They must look different from what we see,
Desirable in some way, otherwise
They'd hardly choose to come here, furtively,
And mutter their bleak needs above the mess
Of fag-ends, crumpled cellophane and crumbs,
Their love feast's litter. Though they might profess
To find great joy together, all that comes
Across to us is tiredness, melancholy.

When they are silent each seems listening;
There must be many voices in the air:
Reproaches, accusations, suffering
That no amount of passion keeps elsewhere.
Imperatives that brought them to this room,
Stiff from the car's back seat, lose urgency;
They start to wonder who's betraying whom,
How it will end, and how did it begin –
The woman taken in adultery
And the man who feels he, too, was taken in.

Vernon Scannell

MARRIAGES CAN GO UP
AS WELL AS DOWN

To profit from a marriage, you have to ride out the peaks
and troughs and the years of recession when your stake
appears worthless – you have to be in it for the long term.
True, familiarity can breed contempt, or rather chronic
low-grade annoyance, but it can also bring the kind of
understanding that Heaney writes about in 'The Skunk'.

Teodoro Luna's Two Kisses

Mr Teodoro Luna in his later years had taken to kissing
His wife
Not so much with his lips as with his brows.
This is not to say he put his forehead
Against her mouth –
Rather, he would lift his eyebrows, once, quickly:
Not so vigorously he might be confused with the villain
Famous in the theatres, but not so little as to be thought
A slight movement, one of accident. This way
He kissed her
Often and quietly, across tables and through doorways,
Sometimes in photographs, and so through the years themselves.
This was his passion, that only she might see. The chance
He might feel some movement on her lips
Toward laughter.

Alberto Rios

Love Poem

My clumsiest dear, whose hands shipwreck vases,
At whose quick touch all glasses chip and ring,
Whose palms are bulls in china, burrs in linen
And have no cunning with any soft thing

Except at ill-at-ease fidgeting people:
The refugee uncertain at the door
You make a steady home; deftly you steady
The drunk clambering on his undulant floor

Unpredictable dear, the taxi driver's terror,
Shrinking from far headlights pale as a dime
Yet leaping before red apoplectic streetcars –
Misfit in any space. And never on time.

A wrench in clocks and the solar system. Only
With words and people and love you move at ease.
In traffic of wit expertly manoeuvre
And keep us, all devotion, at your knees.

Forgetting your coffee spreading on our flannel,
Your lipstick grinning on our coat,
So gaily in love's unbreakable heaven
Our souls on glory of spilt bourbon float.

Be with me, darling, early and late. Smash glasses –
I will study wry music for your sake.
For should your hands drop white and empty
All the toys of the world would break.

John Frederick Nims

The Skunk

Up, black, striped and damasked like the chasuble
At a funeral mass, the skunk's tail
Paraded the skunk. Night after night
I expected her like a visitor.

The refrigerator whinnied into silence.
My desk light softened beyond the verandah.
Small oranges loomed in the orange tree.
I began to be tense as a voyeur.

After eleven years I was composing
Love-letters again, broaching the word 'wife'
Like a stored cask, as if its slender vowel
Had mutated into the night earth and air

Of California. The beautiful, useless
Tang of eucalyptus spelt your absence.
The aftermath of a mouthful of wine
Was like inhaling you off a cold pillow.

And there she was, the intent and glamorous,
Ordinary, mysterious skunk,
Mythologised, demythologised,
Snuffing the boards five feet beyond me.

It all came back to me last night, stirred
By the sootfall of your things at bedtime,
Your head-down, tail-up hunt in a bottom drawer
For the black plunge-line nightdress.

Seamus Heaney

Acknowledgement

When I was lonely
Your fingers reached for mine, their touch
Natural as sunlight's.

When I was hardened
Your warmness thawed my rock as gently
As music thought.

When I was angry
You smiled: 'But this our day is short
For these long shadows.'

When I was solemn
You held out laughter, casual as light
For a cigarette.

When I was troubled
Your understanding crossed the bounds of
Words to silence.

When I was frightened
Your eyes said: 'Fear's a child's dream. I too
Have dreamed and woken.'

A. S. J. Tessimond

In a Bath Teashop

'Let us not speak, for the love we bear one another –
    Let us hold hands and look.'
She, such a very ordinary little woman;
    He, such a thumping crook;
But both, for a moment, little lower than the angels
    In the teashop's ingle-nook.

Sir John Betjeman

Sonnet 29

When in disgrace with fortune and men's eyes
    I all alone beweep my outcast state,
And trouble deaf heaven with my bootless cries,
    And look upon myself, and curse my fate,
Wishing me like to one more rich in hope,
    Featured like him, like him with friends possessed,
Desiring this man's art, and that man's scope,
    With what I most enjoy contented least;
Yet in these thoughts myself almost despising,
    Haply I think on thee, and then my state,
Like to the lark at break of day arising
    From sullen earth, sings hymns at heaven's gate;
For thy sweet love remembered such wealth brings
    That then I scorn to change my state with kings.

William Shakespeare

END GAME

It's not over till it's over, but the end is in sight. Or if not the actual end, at least the end of the illusion. You can accept the bleakness of this situation as Larkin does in 'Talking in Bed':

> It becomes still more difficult to find
> Words at once true and kind,
> Or not untrue and not unkind.

or you can wrap yourself in self-delusion like the narrator of Stevie Smith's 'Infelice'. What you really need is a fast-forward button.

Talking in Bed

Talking in bed ought to be easiest,
Lying together there goes back so far,
An emblem of two people being honest.

Yet more and more time passes silently.
Outside, the wind's incomplete unrest
Builds and disperses clouds about the sky,

And dark towns heap up on the horizon.
None of this cares for us. Nothing shows why
At this unique distance from isolation

It becomes still more difficult to find
Words at once true and kind,
Or not untrue and not unkind.

Philip Larkin

Changing

It occurs to me now,
I never see you smiling
anymore. Friends
Praise your humour rich, your phrases
turning on a thin
dime. For me your wit is honed
to killing sharpness.
But I never catch
you simply smiling, anymore.

Maya Angelou

Ending

The love we thought would never stop
now cools like a congealing chop.
The kisses that were hot as curry
are bird-pecks taken in a hurry.
The hands that held electric charges
now lie inert as four moored barges.
The feet that ran to meet a date
are running slow and running late.
The eyes that shone and seldom shut
are victims of a power cut.
The parts that then transmitted joy
are now reserved and cold and coy.
Romance, expected once to stay,
has left a note saying GONE AWAY.

Gavin Ewart

Infelice

Walking swiftly with a dreadful duchess,
He smiled too briefly, his face was as pale as sand,
He jumped into a taxi when he saw me coming,
Leaving me alone with a private meaning,
He loves me so much, my heart is singing.
Later at the Club when I rang him in the evening
They said: Sir Rat is dining, is dining, is dining,
No Madam, he left no message, ah how his silence speaks,
He loves me too much for words, my heart is singing.
The Pullman seats are here, the tickets for Paris, I am waiting,
Presently the telephone rings, it is his valet speaking,
Sir Rat is called away, to Scotland, his constituents,
(Ah the dreadful duchess, but he loves me the best)
Best pleasure to the last, my heart is singing.
One night he came, it was four in the morning,
Walking slowly upstairs, he stands beside my bed,
Dear darling, lie beside me, it is too cold to stand speaking,
He lies down beside me, his face is like the sand,
He is in a sleep of love, my heart is singing.
Sleeping softly softly, in the morning I must wake him,
And waking he murmurs, I only came to sleep.
The words are so sweetly cruel, how deeply he loves me,
I say them to myself alone, my heart is singing.

Now the sunshine strengthens, it is ten in the morning,
He is so timid in love, he only needs to know,
He is my little child, how can he come if I do not call him,
I will write and tell him everything, I take the pen and write:
I love you so much, my heart is singing.

Stevie Smith

THE SHORT GOODBYE

At times like these, honesty is not the best policy. Better to put a brave face on it, as Maya Angelou does in 'The Lie'. You'll be thankful later.

Parting

Since there's no help, come let us kiss and part –
Nay, I have done, you get no more of me;
And I am glad, yea, glad with all my heart,
That thus so cleanly I myself can free.
Shake hands for ever, cancel all our vows,
And when we meet at any time again,
Be it not seen in either of our brows
Than we one jot of former love retain.
Now at the last gasp of Love's latest breath,
When, his pulse failing, Passion speechless lies,
When Faith is kneeling by his bed of death,
And Innocence is closing up his eyes –
Now if thou would'st, when all have given him over,
From death to life thou might'st him yet recover!

Michael Drayton

The Lie

Today, you threaten to leave me.
I hold curses, in my mouth,
which could flood your path, sear
bottomless chasms in your road.

I keep, behind my lips,
invectives capable of tearing
the septum from your
nostrils and the skin from your back.

Tears, copious as a spring rain,
are checked in ducts
and screams are crowded in a corner
of my throat.

You are leaving?

Aloud, I say:
I'll help you pack, but it's getting late,
I have to hurry or miss my date.
When I return, I know you'll be gone.
Do drop a line or telephone.

Maya Angelou

The End of Love

The end of love should be a big event.
It should involve the hiring of a hall.
Why the hell not? It happens to us all.
Why should it pass without acknowledgement?

Suits should be dry-cleaned, invitations sent.
Whatever form it takes – a tiff, a brawl –
The end of love should be a big event.
It should involve the hiring of a hall.

Better than the unquestioning descent
Into the trap of silence, than the crawl
From visible to hidden, door to wall.

Get the announcement made, the money spent.
The end of love should be a big event.
It should involve the hiring of a hall.

Sophie Hannah

EMPTY BEDS

Although these poems are hardly comforting, the broken hearted may find them consoling. Much classier than getting out the Patsy Cline. Anybody whose friends have tried to cheer them up with homilies along the lines of 'time's a great healer' will sympathise with Edna St Vincent Millay's exasperation when she says:

> Time does not bring relief; you all have lied
> Who told me time would ease me of my pain!

Go Now

Like the touch of the rain she was
On a man's flesh and hair and eyes
When the joy of walking thus
Has taken him by surprise:

With the love of the storm he burns,
He sings, he laughs, well I know how,
But forgets when he returns
As I shall not forget her 'Go now'.

Those two words shut a door
Between me and the blessed rain
That was never shut before
And will not open again.

Edward Thomas

Time does not bring relief

Time does not bring relief; you all have lied
Who told me time would ease me of my pain!
I miss him in the weeping of the rain;
I want him at the shrinking of the tide;
The old snows melt from every mountain-side,
And last year's leaves are smoke in every lane;
But last year's bitter loving must remain
Heaped on my heart, and my old thoughts abide.
There are a hundred places where I fear
To go, – so with his memory they brim.
And entering with relief some quiet place
Where never fell his foot or shone his face
I say, 'There is no memory of him here!'
And so stand stricken, so remembering him.

Edna St Vincent Millay

One Art

The art of losing isn't hard to master;
so many things seem filled with the intent
to be lost that their loss is no disaster.

Lose something every day. Accept the fluster
of lost door keys, the hour badly spent.
The art of losing isn't hard to master.

Then practice losing farther, losing faster:
places, and names, and where it was you meant
to travel. None of these will bring disaster.

I lost my mother's watch. And look! my last, or
next-to-last, of three loved houses went.
The art of losing isn't hard to master.

I lost two cities, lovely ones. And, vaster,
some realms I owned, two rivers, a continent.
I miss them, but it wasn't a disaster.

—Even losing you (the joking voice, a gesture
I love) I shan't have lied. It's evident
the art of losing's not too hard to master
though it may look like (*Write* it!) like disaster.

Elizabeth Bishop

Defining the Problem

I can't forgive you. Even if I could,
You wouldn't pardon me for seeing through you
And yet I cannot cure myself of love
For what I thought you were before I knew you.

Wendy Cope

Coat

Sometimes I have wanted
to throw you off
like a heavy coat.

Sometimes I have said
you would not let me
breathe or move.

But now that I am free
to choose light clothes
or none at all

I feel the cold
and all the time I think
how warm it used to be.

Vicki Feaver

Acquainted with the Night

I have been one acquainted with the night.
I have walked out in the rain – and back in the rain.
I have outwalked the furthest city light.

I have looked down the saddest city lane
I have passed by the watchman on his beat
And dropped my eyes, unwilling to explain.

I have stood still and stopped the sound of feet
When far away an interrupted cry
Came over houses from another street,

But not to call me back or say good-by;
And further still at an unearthly height,
One luminary clock against the sky

Proclaimed the time was neither wrong nor right.
I have been one acquainted with the night.

Robert Frost

GETTING OVER IT

If you are still at the waking up at 4 a.m. stage, wondering what went wrong, then you probably won't be in the mood for these poems. But if you have got to the point where you miss being able to smile more than you miss the one you loved, then you may find something here to make your risorius* twitch.

* smile muscle

Two Cures for Love

1. Don't see him. Don't phone or write a letter.
2. The easy way: get to know him better.

Wendy Cope

Go to Bed with a Cheese and Pickle Sandwich

It is life enhancing
It doesn't chat you up
You have to make it.

A cheese and pickle sandwich
is never disappointing.
You don't lie there thinking:
Am I too fat?
Too fertile?
Too insecure?

Your thoughts are clear,
your choices simple:
to cut in half,
or not to cut in half.
How thin to slice the cheese,
and where you should place the pickle.

From a cheese and pickle sandwich
you do not expect flowers,
poems, and acts of adoration.
You expect what you get:
cheese . . . and pickle.

You want, you eat,
and afterwards you have eaten.
No lying awake resentful,
listening to it snore.

Safe snacks.
It comes recommended.

Mandy Coe

To Rid Myself of You

To rid myself of you
I went and took a shower.
I scoured most carefully
All the places where

You used to hang around.
I unscrewed each ear
And blew through them until
Their galleries were bare.

I took my eyeballs out
And polished them with spit
Until your image fled;
Then to my nostrils put

A little silver drill,
And after I was through
Those passages retained
Nothing at all of you.

So, why is it at night,
When I cannot sleep,
To my nostrils, eyes and ears
Back again you creep?

Alistair Campbell

They Might not Need Me

They might not need me – yet they might –
I'll let my Heart be just in sight –
A smile so small as mine might be
Precisely their necessity –

Emily Dickinson

Loss

The day he moved out was terrible –
That evening she went through hell.
His absence wasn't a problem
But the corkscrew had gone as well.

Wendy Cope

The same hour will not strike

'Nothing happens twice,
And the same rain will not fall,
And the same wind will not pass,'
Said the Lover sadly, sadly,
   Looking at the girl
     Looking in the glass.

'Nothing happens twice,
And the same rain will not fall,
And the same stream will not run,'
Said the Lost One gladly, gladly,
   Groping past the Horror,
     Past the Shadow, to the Sun.

A. S. J. Tessimond

THIS YEAR'S MODEL

Just when you think the Teflon coating is finally in
place, you hear your ex's name in public and it just glides
off – that's when you find out about your replacement.
Rupert Brooke and Eleanor Brown are required reading for
the insanely jealous. Of course, there are some people who
get on famously with their replacements and for them I
include E. E. Cummings's sonnet, 'it may not always be
so;and i say'.

Jealousy

When I see you, who were so wise and cool,
Gazing with silly sickness on that fool
You've given your love to, your adoring hands
Touch his so intimately that each understands,
I know, most hidden things; and when I know
Your holiest dreams yield to that stupid bow
Of his red lips, and that empty grace
Of those strong legs and arms, that rosy face,
Has beaten your heart to such a flame of love,
That you have given him every touch and move,
Wrinkle and secret of you, all your life,
– Oh! then I know I'm waiting, lover-wife,
For the great time when love is at a close,
And all its fruit's to watch the thickening nose
And sweaty neck and dulling face and eye,
That are yours, and you, most surely, till you die!
Day after day you'll sit with him and note
The greasier tie, the dingy wrinkling coat;
As prettiness turns to pomp, and strength to fat,
And love love, love to habit!

                        And after that,
When all that's fine in man is at an end,
And you, that loved young life and clean, must tend
A foul sick fumbling dribbling body and old,
When his rare lips hang flabby and can't hold
Slobber, and you're enduring that worst thing,
Senility's queasy furtive love-making,

And searching those dear eyes for human meaning,
Propping the bald and helpless head, and cleaning
A scrap that life's flung by, and love's forgotten, —
Then you'll be tired; and passion dead and rotten;
And he'll be dirty, dirty!

                    O lithe and free
And lightfoot, that the poor heart cries to see,
That's how I'll see your man and you! —

                              But you
— Oh, when that time comes, you'll be dirty too!

Rupert Brooke

Bitcherel

You ask what I think of your new acquisition;
and since we are now to be 'friends',
I'll strive to the full to cement my position
with honesty. Dear – it depends.

It depends on taste, which must not be disputed;
for which of us *does* understand
why some like their furnishings pallid and muted,
their cookery wholesome, but bland?

There isn't a *law* that a face should have features,
it's just that they generally *do*;
God couldn't give colour to *all* of his creatures,
and only gave wit to a few;

I'm sure she has qualities, much underrated,
that compensate amply for this,
along with a charm that is so understated
it's easy for people to miss.

And if there are some who choose clothing to flatter
what beauties they think they possess,
when what's underneath has no shape, does it matter
if there is no shape to the dress?

It's not that I think she is *boring*, precisely,
that isn't the word I would choose;
I know there are men who like girls who talk nicely
and always wear sensible shoes.

It's not that I think she is vapid and silly;
it's not that her voice makes me wince;
But – chilli con carne without any chilli
is only a plateful of mince . . .

Eleanor Brown

The Sending of Five

Five potent curses
I send, the first
Love, which frequently
Drives men to suffer
Uncouth hair transplants.

The second, riches,
Bringing in their train
The envy of friends
Expressed in these words:
'It's all right for some.'

My third curse is fame:
May you become sport
For reporters, may
The dull quote you, may
Cranks think they are you.

My fourth, contentment,
Hugging you, white grub,
In a fat cocoon
That the cries of men
Cannot penetrate.

And last, a long life.
May you live to be
Called 'The Grand Old Man.'
Smiling at you, may
The young sprain their jaws.

Vicki Raymond

it may not always be so;and i say

it may not always be so;and i say
that if your lips,which i have loved,should touch
another's,and your dear strong fingers clutch
his heart,as mine in time not far away;
if on another's face your sweet hair lay
in such a silence as i know,or such
great writhing words as,uttering overmuch,
stand helplessly before the spirit at bay;

if this should be,i say if this should be—
you of my heart, send me a little word;
that i may go unto him,and take his hands,
saying,Accept all happiness from me.
Then shall i turn my face,and hear one bird
sing terribly afar in the lost lands.

E. E. Cummings

FOR OLD TIMES' SAKE

When the worst of it is over, you have two options:
acrimonious reunions as portrayed by James Fenton in his
parody of Auld Lang Syne, or you can take Fleur Adcock's
advice in her poem, 'Happy Ending':

> they giggled, reminisced, held hands
> as though what they had made was love –
> and not that happier outcome, friends.

Let's Go Over It All Again

Some people are like that.
They split up and then they think:
Hey, maybe we haven't hurt each other to the uttermost.
Let's meet up and have a drink

Let's go over it all again
Let's rake over the dirt.
Let me pick that scab of yours.
Does it hurt?

Let's go over what went wrong –
How and why and when.
Let's go over what went wrong
Again and again.

We hurt each other badly once.
We said a lot of nasty stuff.
But lately I've been thinking how
I didn't hurt you enough.

Maybe there's more where that came from,
Something more malign.
Let me damage you again
For the sake of auld lang syne.

Yes, let me see you bleed again
For the sake of auld lang syne.

James Fenton

Happy Ending

After they had not made love
she pulled the sheet up over her eyes
until he was buttoning his shirt:
not shyness for their bodies – those
they had willingly displayed – but a frail
endeavour to apologise.

Later, though, drawn together by
a distaste for such 'untidy ends'
they agreed to meet again; whereupon
they giggled, reminisced, held hands
as though what they had made was love –
and not that happier outcome, friends.

Fleur Adcock

LOST FOR EVER

The poems here all are trying to contain the most chaotic emotion – grief. Emily Dickinson's punctuation, 'First Chill – then Stupor – then the letting go –', is a literal representation of the incoherence of bereavement. The Auden poem is justly famous, but I find the C. S. Lewis poem the more poignant. The poem is undated but it was almost certainly written in the period when his wife Joy was dying of cancer. The title refers to his wife, but also to his belief that his own osteoporosis was the price he had to pay for a brief period of remission in Joy's disease. As he wrote to a friend, 'I was losing calcium just about as fast as Joy was gaining it, a bargain (if it was one) for which I am very thankful.'

Joys That Sting

Oh doe not die says Donne, *for I shall hate*
All women so. How false the sentence rings.
Women? But in a life made desolate
It is the joys once shared that have the stings.

To take the old walks alone, or not at all,
To order one pint when I ordered two,
To think of and then not to make, the small
Time-honoured joke (senseless to all but you);

To laugh (oh, one'll laugh), to talk upon
Themes that we talked upon when you were there,
To make some small pretence of going on,
Be kind to one's old friends, and seem to care,

While no one (O God) through the years will say
The simplest, common word in just your way.

C. S. Lewis

Love in a Life

I

Room after room,
I hunt the house through
We inhabit together.
Heart, fear nothing, for, heart, thou shalt find her –
Next time, herself! – not the trouble behind her
Left in the curtain, the couch's perfume!
As she brushed it, the cornice-wreath blossomed anew:
Yon looking-glass gleamed at the wave of her feather.

II

Yet the day wears,
And door succeeds door;
I try the fresh fortune –
Range the wide house from the wing to the centre.
Still the same chance! she goes out as I enter.
Spend my whole day in the quest, – who cares?
But 'tis twilight, you see – with such suites to explore,
Such closets to search, such alcoves to importune!

Robert Browning

Funeral Blues

Stop all the clocks, cut off the telephone,
Prevent the dog from barking with a juicy bone,
Silence the pianos and with muffled drum
Bring out the coffin, let the mourners come.

Let aeroplanes circle moaning overhead
Scribbling on the sky the message He Is Dead,
Put crêpe bows round the white necks of the public doves,
Let the traffic policemen wear black cotton gloves.

He was my North, my South, my East and West,
My working week and my Sunday rest,
My noon, my midnight, my talk, my song;
I thought that love would last forever: I was wrong.

The stars are not wanted now: put out every one;
Pack up the moon and dismantle the sun;
Pour away the ocean and sweep up the wood,
For nothing now can ever come to any good.

W. H. Auden

Sonnet

Surprised by joy – impatient as the wind
I turned to share the transport – Oh! with whom
But thee, deep buried in the silent tomb,
That spot which no vicissitude can find?
Love, faithful love, recalled thee to my mind –
But how could I forget thee? Through what power,
Even for the least division of an hour,
Have I been so beguiled as to be blind
To my most grievous loss! – That thought's return
Was the worst pang that sorrow ever bore,
Save one, one only, when I stood forlorn,
Knowing my heart's best treasure was no more;
That neither present time, nor years unborn
Could to my sight that heavenly face restore.

William Wordsworth

After Great Pain

After great pain, a formal feeling comes –
The Nerves sit ceremonious, like Tombs –
The stiff Heart questions was it He, that bore,
And Yesterday, or Centuries before?

The Feet, mechanical, go round –
Of Ground, or Air, or Ought –
A Wooden way
Regardless grown,
A Quartz contentment, like a stone –

This is the Hour of Lead –
Remembered, if outlived,
As Freezing persons, recollect the Snow –
First – Chill – then Stupor – then the letting go –

Emily Dickinson

A Marriage

We met
   under a shower
of bird-notes.
   Fifty years passed,
love's moment
   in a world in
servitude to time.
   She was young;
I kissed with my eyes
   closed and opened
them on her wrinkles.
   'Come,' said death,
choosing her as his
   partner for the last
dance. And she,
   who in life
had done everything
   with a bird's grace,
opened her bill now
   for the shedding
of one sigh no
   heavier than a feather.

R. S. Thomas

YOU CAN RUN . . .

We can be as ruthless as we like with our past, razing
the emotional detritus with flame throwers of contempt –
'What on earth was I thinking of!' But can one entirely
avoid those unexpected encounters with past passion
which make the heart thud, as Carol Ann Duffy puts it, 'like
a spade on buried bones'.

The Darling *Letters*

Some keep them in shoeboxes away from the light,
sore memories blinking as the lid lifts,
their own recklessnesses written all over them. *My own . . .*
Private jokes, no longer comprehended, pull their punchlines,
fall flat in the gaps between endearments. *What
are you wearing?*

                Don't ever change.
They start with *Darling*; end in recriminations,
absence, sense of loss. Even now, the fist's bud flowers
into trembling, the fingers trace each line and see
The future then. *Always . . .* Nobody burns them,
the *Darling* letters, stiff in their cardboard coffins.

Babykins . . . We all had strange names
which make us blush, as though we'd murdered
someone under an alias, long ago. *I'll die
without you. Die.* Once in a while, alone,
we take them out to read again, the heart thudding
like a spade on buried bones.

Carol Ann Duffy

When We Two Parted

When we two parted
　In silence and tears,
Half broken-hearted
　To sever for years,
Pale grew thy cheek and cold,
　Colder thy kiss;
Truly that hour foretold
　Sorrow to this.

The dew of the morning
　Sunk chill on my brow –
It felt like a warning
　Of what I feel now.
Thy vows are all broken,
　And light is thy fame:
I hear thy name spoken,
　And share in its shame.

They name thee before me,
　A knell to mine ear;
A shudder comes o'er me –
　Why wert thou so dear?
They know not I knew thee,
　Who knew thee too well: –
Long, long shall I rue thee,
　Too deeply to tell.

In secret we met –
    In silence I grieve,
That thy heart could forget,
    Thy spirit deceive.
If I should meet thee
    After long years,
How should I greet thee! –
    With silence and tears.

Lord Byron

When You Are Old

When you are old and gray and full of sleep
   And nodding by the fire, take down this book,
   And slowly read, and dream of the soft look
Your eyes had once, and of their shadows deep;

How many loved your moments of glad grace,
   And loved your beauty with love false or true;
   But one man loved the pilgrim soul in you,
And loved the sorrows of your changing face.

And bending down beside the glowing bars,
   Murmur, a little sadly, how love fled
   And paced upon the mountains overhead,
And hid his face amid a crowd of stars.

W. B. Yeats

SENIOR MOMENTS

There is nothing more revolting to the young than the thought of middle-aged hanky-panky. What they do not realise is that while the face may need a lift, the emotions remain relentlessly perky. You may have crow's-feet instead of acne, but the fourteen-year-old never really goes away. As the North American poet Adrienne Rich writes at the ripe old age of forty-five:

> Did I ever walk the morning streets at twenty,
> my limbs streaming with a purer joy?

from *Twenty-one Love Poems*

Since we're not young, weeks have to do time
for years of missing each other. Yet only this odd warp
in time tells me we're not young.
Did I ever walk the morning streets at twenty,
my limbs streaming with a purer joy?
Did I lean from any window over the city
listening for the future
as I listen here with nerves tuned for your ring?
And you, you move toward me with the same tempo.
Your eyes are everlasting, the green spark
of the blue-eyed grass of early summer,
the green-blue wild cress washed by the spring.
At twenty, yes: we thought we'd live forever.
At forty-five, I want to know even our limits.
I touch you knowing we weren't born tomorrow,
and somehow, each of us will help the other live,
and somewhere, each of us must help the other die.

Adrienne Rich

Love: Beginnings

They're at the stage where so much desire steams between them,
    so much frank need and want,
so much absorption in the other and the self and the self-admiring
    entity and unity they make –
her mouth so full, breast so lifted, head thrown back *so* far
    in her laughter at his laughter,
he so solid, planted, oaky, firm, so resonantly factual in the
    headiness of being craved so,
she almost wreathed upon him as they intertwine again, touch
    again, cheek, lip, shoulder, brow,
every glance moving toward the sexual, every glance away soaring
    back in the flame into the sexual –
that just to watch them is to feel that hitching in the groin,
    that filling of the heart,
the old, sore heart, the battered, foundered, faithful heart,
    snorting again, stamping in its stall.

C. K. Williams

A Decade

When you came, you were like red wine and honey,
And the taste of you burnt my mouth with its sweetness.
Now you are like morning bread.
Smooth and pleasant.
I hardly taste you at all for I know your savour.
But I am completely nourished.

Amy Lowell

THE LAST DETAIL

If you have read the last third of this book with recognition – if you have even a passing acquaintance with heartbreak – you will have wondered whether love should be labelled a Class A drug: highly addictive and fatal in its purest form. But, as the wonderful Greek poet C. P. Cavafy reminds us in 'Valedictory', the journey is more important than reaching the destination. Every experience, however painful, has its reward.

The final poem was written by the American poet and short story writer, Raymond Carver, after he was diagnosed with an inoperable brain tumour, for his second wife Tess Gallagher. Carver's first marriage had been tempestuously unhappy and had left him alcoholic and unable to write. It was only when he met Tess that he stopped drinking and began to write again. His happiness was short-lived, but as 'Late Fragment' shows, it was worth it.

Valedictory (from *Ithaka*)

As you set out for Ithaka
hope your road is a long one,
full of adventure, full of discovery . . .

Keep Ithaka always in your mind.
Arriving there is what you're destined for.
But don't hurry the journey at all.
Better if it lasts for years,
so you're old by the time you reach the island,
wealthy with all you've gained on the way,
not expecting Ithaka to make you rich.

Ithaka gave you the marvellous journey.
Without her you wouldn't have set out.
She has nothing left to give you now.

And if you find her poor, Ithaka won't have fooled you.
Wise as you will have become, so full of experience,
you'll have understood by then what these Ithakas mean.

C. P. Cavafy

Dover Beach

The sea is calm to-night.
The tide is full, the moon lies fair
Upon the Straits; – on the French coast, the light
Gleams and is gone; the cliffs of England stand,
Glimmering and vast, out in the tranquil bay.
Come to the window, sweet is the night air!
Only, from the long line of spray
Where the ebb meets the moon-blanch'd land,
Listen! you hear the grating roar
Of pebbles which the waves draw back, and fling,
At their return, up the high strand,
Begin, and cease, and then again begin,
With tremulous cadence slow, and bring
The eternal note of sadness in.

Sophocles long ago
Heard it on the Aegean, and it brought
Into his mind the turbid ebb and flow
Of human misery; we
Find also in the sound a thought,
Hearing it by this distant northern sea.

The Sea of faith
Was once, too, at the full, and round earth's shore
Lay like the folds of a bright girdle furl'd;
But now I only hear
Its melancholy, long, withdrawing roar,
Retreating, to the breath
Of the night-wind, down the vast edges drear
And naked shingles of the world.

Ah, love, let us be true
To one another! for the world, which seems
To lie before us like a land of dreams,
So various, so beautiful, so new,
Hath really neither joy, nor love, nor light,
Nor certitude, nor peace, nor help for pain;
And we are here as on a darkling plain
Swept with confused alarms of struggle and flight,
Where ignorant armies clash by night.

Matthew Arnold

Late Fragment

And did you get what
you wanted from this life, even so?
I did.
And what did you want?
To call myself beloved, to feel myself
beloved on the earth.

Raymond Carver

AUTHOR BIOGRAPHIES

FLEUR ADCOCK (1934–)
New Zealand poet and translator. Born in Papakura, her family moved to England when she was five although returned after World War II when she was 13. She returned to settle in Britain in 1963 after she divorced fellow New Zealand poet, Alistair Campbell. Her books include *Tigers* (1967), *High Tide in the Garden* (1971) and *The Incident Book* (1986).

ALVARO (1943–)
The poet, singer, and songwriter Alvaro Peña-Rojas was born in Valparaíso, Chile. He currently resides in Germany.

MAYA ANGELOU (1928–)
Born in St Louis, Missouri, as Marguerite Johnson, she has written numerous volumes of autobiography and poetry, including *I Know Why the Caged Bird Sings* (1970) and *On the Pulse of Morning* (1993), the poem she read at President Clinton's inauguration.

MATTHEW ARNOLD (1822–88)
British poet and critic. Born at Laleham-on-Thames, Surrey, Arnold's work included *Empedocles on Etna, and Other Poems* (1852), *Poems* (1853) and *Poems, Second Series* (1855). He was an inspector of schools between 1851 and 1883. He died of a heart attack on 15 April 1888 and was buried in the town where he was born.

MARGARET (ELEANOR) ATWOOD (1939–)
Canadian novelist, critic, short-story writer and poet. Born in Ottawa, her poetry collections include *The Circle Game* (1966), *Power Politics* (1971), *You Are Happy* (1974), *Interlunar* (1988) and *Morning in the Burned House* (1995).

W. H. (WYSTAN HUGH) AUDEN (1907–73)
British left-wing poet, dramatist and librettist. *Look, Stranger!* (1936) is the volume of poetry that secured Auden's poetical reputation. He emigrated to America in 1939 where he wrote *The Age of Anxiety* (1947), which won him the Pulitzer Prize.

CONNIE BENSLEY (1929–)
British poet. Born in London. Her latest collection is *The Back and the Front of It* (2002), published by Bloodaxe Books.

SIR JOHN BETJEMAN (1906–84)
British poet. Born in Highgate, London, Betjeman worked variously as a film critic for the *Evening Standard*, an architecture critic and as a Press Officer in Dublin to the

British representative. The IRA thought he was a spy and considered assassinating him. He suffered from Parkinson's disease later in life.

EARLE BIRNEY (1904–95)
Canadian poet. Born in Calgary, Alberta, he twice received the Governor General's Award for Literature, in 1942 and 1945.

ELIZABETH BISHOP (1911–79)
Born in Massachusetts. After travelling in Europe and North Africa between 1935–37, she spent 15 years in Brazil where she lived with her lover, Lota. In her later years she moved back to Massachusetts to teach at Harvard, suffering from alcoholism and depression. Her work includes *North and South* (1946); *Geography III* (1976) and *Complete Poems 1927–1979* (1983), published after her death.

WILLIAM BLAKE (1757–1827)
British poet and artist. Born in London, he married an illiterate woman named Catherine Boucher, whom he taught to read and write. His most popular collection, *Songs of Innocence*, appeared in 1789, followed by *Songs of Experience* (1794).

NINA BOURNE (1916–)
Bourne has worked in publishing since 1939, first for Simon & Schuster then for Alfred A. Knopf. *Where the Single Men Go in Summer* was first published in *The New Yorker*.

RUPERT (CHAWNER) BROOKE (1887–1915)
English poet. Born in Rugby, Warwickshire. Though known as a war poet, strictly speaking Brooke was a Georgian poet with a broad range of poetical subject matter – from imagining the world from a fish's point-of-view to the growing old disgracefully of 'Menelaus and Helen'. He died on a hospital ship off the island of Scyros during World War I of septicaemia resulting from a mosquito bite.

ELEANOR BROWN (1969–)
English poet. After working variously as a barmaid and legal secretary, she took up her present post of Writing Fellow at the University of Strathclyde. Her first collection *Maiden Speech* (1997) was shortlisted for the *Mail on Sunday*/John Llewellyn Rhys Prize.

ROBERT BROWNING (1812–89)
British poet born in Camberwell, London, he married poet Elizabeth Barrett Browning with whom he had established a literary correspondence. They eloped in 1846. Browning wrote prolifically – 'Sordello and The Ring' and 'The Book' number among his many works. On the day of his death in December 1889, his last poems were published.

CHARLES BUKOWSKI (1920–94)
American poet. Born in Andernach, Germany, before moving to America at the age of three. He started writing poetry at the age of 35. He worked in a post office between 1958 and 1969

before deciding to make a career as a writer. A prolific poet, his work includes *The Last Night of the Earth Poems* (1992*), You Get So Alone At Times That It Just Makes Sense* (1986) and *The Roominghouse Madrigals: Early Selected Poems, 1946–1966* (1988).

ROBERT BURNS (1759–96)
Scottish poet. His work includes *Poems Chiefly in the Scottish Dialect* (1786) and poems such as *Tam O'Shanter* (1791). He also collected numerous traditional Scottish songs for *The Scots Musical Museum* (1787–1803) in which he reworked ballads such as 'Auld Lang Syne'. He worked as an excise official from 1791 until his death in 1796 of rheumatic fever.

LORD (GEORGE GORDON) BYRON (1788–1824)
British poet. Born in London, but because of rumours of incest with his half-sister Augusta Leigh and rising debts, he left England in 1816 never to return. Byron was famous for his womanising. Lady Caroline Lamb – with whom he had an affair – coined the phrase famously used to describe Byron, saying he was 'Mad, bad and dangerous to know'.

ALISTAIR (TE ARIKI) CAMPBELL (1926–)
New Zealand novelist, playwright and poet. He was born in the Cook Islands where he spent the first seven years of his life. He fought in World War I, before becoming an island storekeeper. He married poet Fleur Adcock, but they divorced and he then married actress Meg Anderson

in 1958. His work includes *Dreams, Yellow Lions* (1975), *Dark Lord of Savaiki* (1980), *Collected Poems* (1981) and *Soul Traps* (1985).

RAYMOND CARVER (1938–88)
American short-story writer and poet. Born in Clatskanie, Oregon. His work has been translated into more than 20 languages. He married at the age of 19, and had two children by the time he was 21. He was hospitalised four times in 1976 and 1977 for his acute alcoholism, which almost killed him.

C. P. (CONSTANTINE PETER) CAVAFY (1863–1933)
Poet. Born in Alexandria, Egypt, he published his first volume of poems privately in 1904 and all his poems thereafter were circulated on broadsheets only to his friends. His collected work appeared in 1935 – two years after his death.

JOHN CLARE (1793–1864)
British poet. Born in Northamptonshire, the self-educated son of a labourer, none of Clare's later work matched up to the critical acclaim his first book received – *Poems Descriptive of Rural Life and Scenery* (1820). He was certified as insane in 1837 and spent the rest of his life in an asylum.

MANDY COE (1962–)
Born in London, Coe currently resides in Aigburth, Liverpool. She is a visual artist as well as a poet. She also runs writing workshops in schools and community centres. Her most

recent collection is *Pinning the Tail on the Donkey* (2000).

WENDY COPE (1945–)
British poet, whose books include *Making Cocoa for Kingsley Amis* (1986) and *Serious Concerns* (1992). Cope trained as a teacher and worked as a television columnist for *The Spectator* between 1986 and 1990.

E. E. (EDWARD ESTLIN) CUMMINGS (1894–1962)
American novelist, playwright and poet. Born in Cambridge, Massachusetts, Cummings prized individuality and immediate emotional response above intellect and intellectual understanding. In 1932 he married Marion Morehouse with whom he collaborated on *Adventures in Value* (1962). He wrote a large number of poems, including 'i sing of olaf glad and big', 'buffalo bill' and 'may i feel'.

CECIL DAY-LEWIS (1904–72)
Anglo-Irish poet and critic. Born in Ballintubbert, Co Laois, Cecil Day-Lewis was appointed Poet Laureate in 1968. As well as writing poetry, Day-Lewis also wrote detective fiction under the pseudonym Nicholas Blake. He married twice and had five children, one of whom is the actor Daniel Day-Lewis.

EMILY DICKINSON (1830–86)
American poet. Born in Amherst, Massachusetts, the town where she spent her entire life, she wrote over 1,700 poems, though only 10 of these poems were published during her lifetime. Her sister found and published her work after her death.

MOYRA DONALDSON (1956–)
Irish poet. Born in Co Down, She is currently literary editor of the political Belfast *Fortnight Magazine*. She has published three collections of poetry: *Kissing Ghosts* (1995), *Snakeskin Stilletos* (1999) and *Beneath the Ice (2002)*.

JOHN DONNE (1572–1631)
English metaphysical poet. Born in London, he studied at Hart Hall (Hertford College) in Oxford for three years from the age of 11 before studying for another three years at Cambridge University. Arguably the best known of the metaphysical poets.

MICHAEL DRAYTON (1563–1631)
British poet. Born at Hartshill in Warwickshire, Drayton's first published work was a *Harmonie of the Church* (1591), which turned passages of scripture into highly alliterative verse. Some critics have argued that 'Parting' (taken from his sonnet sequence *Idea*) was inspired by Sir Henry Goodeere of Polesworth's daughter – Anne Goodeere.

CAROL ANN DUFFY (1955–)
British poet and playwright. Her work includes *Standing Female Nude* (1985), *Mean Time* (1993), *Selected Poems* (1995) and *Feminine Gospels* (2002).

ELIZABETH I (1533–1603)
Queen of England. As well as being a great patron of the arts, Elizabeth wrote several poems herself, including 'Written with a Diamond' and 'In Defiance of Fortune'. Her father, King Henry VIII, also wrote a number of poems in his lifetime.

GAVIN (BUCHANAN) EWART (1916–96)
British poet. He first published poems at the age of 17. After serving in the Royal Artillery between 1940–46, he worked for the British Council and then became an advertising copywriter until 1971. He subsequently became a full-time freelance writer.

VICKI FEAVER (1943–)
British poet. Born in Nottingham, her work includes *Close Relatives* (1981) and the *Handless Maiden* (1994). She currently teaches creative writing in Chichester, where she lives with her psychiatrist husband.

JAMES FENTON (1949–)
Poet and reporter. Born in Durham, England, his work includes *Terminal Moraine* (1972), *The Memory of War* (1982), *Manila Envelope* (1989), *Partingtime Hall* (1987), written with John Fuller, and *Out of Danger* (1993). He has also worked as a political and literary journalist.

ROBERT FROST (1874–1963)
American poet. Born in San Francisco, he worked variously as a teacher, cobbler and, in Massachusetts, editor of the Lawrence *Sentinel*. His poem

'The Road Not Taken' was voted America's favourite poem.

KAHLIL GIBRAN (1883–1931)
Lebanese poet. Born in Bisharri, Lebanon, he emigrated at the age of 12 to the United States. He published numerous books, including the phenomenally successful epic poem *The Prophet*. He died of cirrhosis of the liver during Prohibition.

PAMELA GILLILAN (1918–2001)
British poet. Although Gillilan had written poetry from an early age, it was not until the death of her husband David Gillilan in 1974 at the age of 60 that she started to receive literary recognition. She won the Cheltenham literary festival prize in 1979 with her poem 'Come Away', an elegy on the death of her husband. She refused to publicly disclose her age until her 80th birthday.

ROBERT (RANKE) GRAVES (1895–1985)
British poet and novelist. He emigrated to Majorca in 1929. *Goodbye to All That* (1929), Graves's World War I autobiography, established him as a writer. Subsequent work includes his historical novels *I, Claudius* (1934) and *Claudius the God* (1934), his study of mythology *The White Goddess* (1948) and several editions of his *Collected Poems*.

SOPHIE HANNAH (1971–)
British poet and novelist. Born in Manchester where she currently teaches at Manchester Metropolitan University's Writing School. Her

work includes *Gripless* (1999), *Cordial and Corrosive* (2000) and *The Superpower of Love* (2001). Her poetry includes the Arts Council award-winning *Hotels Like Houses* (1996) and *Leaving and Leaving You* (1999).

SEAMUS HEANEY (1939–)
Irish poet. Born in Co Derry, Northern Ireland, he won the Nobel Prize for Literature in 1995. His poetry collections include *The Haw Lantern* (1987), *Seeing Things* (1991) and *Electric Light* (2001).

HEINRICH HEINE (1797–1856)
Poet, prose-writer, critic and journalist. Best known for his *Buch der Lieder [Book of Songs]* (1827) on which Schumann based his *Dichterliebe* (*The Poet's Love*). Heine's work attracted many composers besides Schumann, including Mendelssohn, Brahms, Wolf and Richard Strauss.

GERARD MANLEY HOPKINS (1844–89)
English poet. Hopkins converted to Catholicism in 1866 and became a Jesuit two years later. His work was published posthumously by his friend Robert Bridges in *Collected Poems* (1918).

HELENE JOHNSON (1907–95)
American poet, born in Boston, Massachusetts. One of the youngest poets of the Harlem Renaissance. After a brief spell of literary celebrity she disappeared from the public stage and for the next 50 years wrote only for herself.

ERICA JONG (1942–)
American poet, novelist and critic. She has written eight novels, including *Fear of Flying* (1973), and published six volumes of poetry, including *Fruits & Vegetables* and *Half-Lives.* She lives in New York City and Weston, Connecticut.

PHILIP LARKIN (1922–85)
British poet. Born in Coventry, Larkin worked as a librarian variously at the University of Leicester and Queen's University Belfast. He was a great jazz aficionado and reviewed for the *Daily Telegraph*.

D. H. (DAVID HERBERT) LAWRENCE (1885–1930)
British poet and novelist. Born in Nottingham, in 1912 he met and subsequently married Frieda von Richthofen, his French professor's wife. He died in Venice in 1930.

C. S. (CLIVE STAPLES) LEWIS (1898–1963)
British writer. Born in Belfast in 1898, Clive Staples Lewis fought in World War I and was wounded. During the war he promised a young man he was fighting with that if he died, he would support his mother. Lewis kept his promise. His most famous works are probably *The Screwtape Letters* and *The Chronicles of Narnia*.

LIZ LOCHHEAD (1947–)
Scottish poet and playwright. Born in Motherwell. Her poetry collections include *True Confessions and New Clichés* (1985) and *Bagpipe Muzak* (1991).

AMY (LAWRENCE) LOWELL
(1874–1925)
American poet and critic. Born in
Brookline, Massachusetts. Her first
volume of poetry, *A Dome of Many-
Colored Glass* (1912), was written
before she discovered Imagism in
January 1913, an influence that
dominates her subsequent work. Her
later work included collections such
as *Can Grande's Castle* (1918), *Legends*
(1921) and Pulitzer prize-winning
What's O'Clock (1925). Personally,
Lowell cut an eccentric figure who
stopped clocks, covered mirrors in
her house and enjoyed smoking
cigars.

ANDREW MARVELL (1621–78)
British metaphysical poet. Marvell
was born in Winestead-in-
Holderness in 1621. His work includes
'Upon Appleton House', 'The
Garden', and his most famous poem,
'To his Coy Mistress'.

GLYN MAXWELL (1962–)
British poet, novelist and playwright.
Born in Welwyn Garden City, his
work includes *The Breakage* (1999)
and *Time's Fool* (2001).

ROGER McGOUGH (1937–)
British poet. His books include
Watchword (1969), *Gig* (1972), *Waving
at Trains* (1982), *The Stowaways*
(1986), *An Imaginary Menagerie*
(1988) and *Eclipse* (2002).

EDNA ST VINCENT MILLAY
(1892–1950)
American playwright, novelist and
poet. Born in Maine, she wrote
fiction under the pseudonym Nancy

Boyce. She won the Pulitzer Prize in
1923 for *The Harp-Weaver and Other
Poems*.

ADRIAN MITCHELL (1932–)
British novelist, poet and playwright.
Born in London, he has written
numerous volumes of poetry,
including *Heart on the Left* (1997) and
All Shook Up (2001).

EDWIN MUIR (1887–1959)
Scottish poet and translator. Born
in Orkney, he married the novelist
Willa Anderson and moved to
Prague in the 1930s where he
translated Kafka, among other
writers. His best known works
include *The Voyage* (1946) and *The
Labyrinth* (1949).

JOHN FREDERICK NIMS (1913–99)
American poet and translator. Born
in Muskegon, Michigan. His poetry
includes *Zany in Denim* (1990) and
*The Six-Cornered Snowflake and
Other Poems* (1990). He was editor of
Poetry magazine from 1978 to 1984.

ROSEMARY NORMAN (1946–)
British poet. Born in London. Her
first collection, *Threats and Promises*,
was published in 1991.

FRANK (MICHAEL DONOVAN)
O'CONNOR (1903–66)
Born and brought up in Cork.
Playwright, translator and novelist
best known for his short stories,
particularly *Guests of the Nation*
(1931), which made his name as
a writer. He was a friend of
W. B. Yeats.

DOROTHY PARKER (1893–1967)
Short-story writer, humorist and poet. Born in West End, New Jersey. Her poetry collections include *Enough Rope* (1927) and *Death and Taxes* (1931). She was part of the Algonquin Round Table, a group of New York writers who met at the Algonquin Hotel in the 1920s.

MARGE PIERCY (1936–)
American novelist, essayist and poet. Her writing explores feminism and femininity. Her work includes the novels *Small Changes* (1973), *Woman on the Edge of Time* (1976) and *He, She and It* (1991).

SYLVIA PLATH (1932–63)
American poet born in Jamaica Plain, Massachusetts, who published her first poem when she was eight. She married the British poet Ted Hughes in 1956. Her work includes *The Colossus (1960), Ariel (1965), Crossing the Water (1971), Winter Trees (1981)* and her autobiographical novel *The Bell Jar* published in 1963 – the year she committed suicide.

SHEENAGH PUGH (1950–)
Welsh poet and translator. Pugh currently resides in Cardiff with her husband, two children and cats. She works as a freelance writer as well as teaching creative writing at the University of Glamorgan. Her work includes *Beware Falling Tortoises* (1987), *Selected Poems* (1990) and *Stonelight* (1999).

VICKI RAYMOND (1950–)
Australian poet. Born in Australia, she moved to Tasmania then London, where she married. She currently teaches in London.

CHRISTOPHER REID (1949–)
British poet. Born in Hong Kong in 1949, his work includes *Katerina Brac* (1985), *Expanded Universes* (1996) and *Mermaids Explained: Poems* (2001).

ADRIENNE (CECILE) RICH (1929–)
American poet. Born in Baltimore, Maryland, her work includes *The Diamond Cutters* (1955), *Snapshots of a Daughter-in-Law* (1963), *Necessities of Life* (1966), *A Wild Patience Has Taken Me This Far* (1981) and *An Atlas of the Difficult World* (1991). Her collections *Will to Change* (1971) and *Diving into the Wreck* (1973), published after the death of her husband, established her as a powerful feminist voice.

ALBERTO RIOS (1952–)
Poet brought up in Nogales, Arizona, on the Mexican-American border. His father was from Tapachula, Chiapas, in Mexico and his mother from Warrington in Lancashire, England. His poetry collections include *The Lime Orchard Woman* (1988) and *Teodoro Luna's Two Kisses* (1990).

CARL (AUGUST) SANDBURG (1878–1967)
American Chicago-born novelist and poet. At 17 he travelled across America to Kansas as a hobo, an experience he used as the basis for

many of his subsequent poems. His work includes *Chicago Poems* (1916), *Cornhuskers* (1918), *Good Morning America* (1928) and *Complete Poems* (1950).

VERNON SCANNELL (1922–)
Scannell joined the army at the age of 18, fought and was wounded during the Second World War. He deserted when the war with the Germans was finished because, 'The Far East was not my concern.' He has led a varied and diverse life, earning a living as a boxer and tutor, among other things. His work includes his autobiography *The Tiger and the Rose* (1983), *Collected Poems 1950–93* (1994), *Drums of Morning* (1999) and *Of Love and War* (2002).

PERCY BYSSHE SHELLEY (1792–1822)
English poet. Born in Horsham, Sussex. He married Mary Wollstonecraft (author of *Frankenstein*) in 1816. Shelley's most famous poems include 'Ode to the West Wind', 'Queen Mab: A philosophical poem', and 'Alastor'. Shelley died in a yachting accident in 1822 at the age of 30.

EDWARD ROWLAND SILL (1841–87)
Born in Windsor, Connecticut, Edward Rowland Sill was Professor of English at the University of California between 1874–82. His works include *The Hermitage* (1868) and *Venus of Milo* (1882).

WILLIAM SHAKESPEARE (1564–1616)
English poet and playwright born in Stratford-upon-Avon. His plays include *King Lear*, *Hamlet* and *Romeo and Juliet*, amongst numerous others. He is also famed for his sonnet sequence, which includes meditations on his own fame and mortality.

STEVIE SMITH (1902–71)
British poet and broadcaster. Born Florence Margaret Smith in Hull, in 1969 she won the Queen's Gold Medal for poetry. She published eight volumes of poetry and three novels.

WALLACE STEVENS (1879–1955)
American Poet. Born in Reading, Pennsylvania. He worked as a lawyer for an insurance firm, becoming vice-president of the company in 1934. Most of his poetry was written after the age of 50. His published work includes *Harmonium* (1923), *Man with the Blue Guitar and Other Poems* (1937) and *Collected Poems* (1954).

LUCY SWEETMAN
Runner-up to the Guardian text message poetry competition.

SARA TEASDALE (1884–1933)
American poet, born in St Louis, Missouri. Her work included *Helen of Troy and Other Poems* (1911), *Rivers to the Sea* (1915), *Flame and Shadow* (1920) and *Strange Victory* (1933). Teasdale committed suicide at the age of 48.

ALFRED LORD TENNYSON (1809–92)
Born in Somersby, Lincolnshire. He was appointed Poet Laureate in 1850 on the death of Wordsworth. His best known work includes poems such as 'Maud', 'The Lotos-Eaters', 'The Lady of Shalott', 'The Charge of the

Light Brigade' and 'The Idylls of the King'.

A. S. J. (ARTHUR SEYMOUR JOHN) TESSIMOND (1902–62)
Tessimond was born in Birkenhead, and he published three volumes of poetry during his life. He worked in bookshops and then as an advertising copywriter.

EDWARD (PHILIP) THOMAS (1878–1917)
English poet and journalist. Born in Lambeth, London, Thomas started writing poetry in 1912 under the pseudonym Edward Eastaway, but a meeting with the poet Robert Frost in 1913 inspired him to concentrate more fully on his poems.

R. S. (RONALD STUART) THOMAS (1913–2000)
Welsh poet. Born in Cardiff in 1913, he received theological training before becoming ordained in 1936 and holding various curacies. He married the painter Mildred E. Eldridge, whose death is the subject of 'A Marriage'. The poem appears in his *A Mass for Hard Times* (1993).

ROSEMARY TONKS (1932–)
British poet. Born in London in 1932, she published two collections of poetry in the 1960s, *Notes on cafes and bedrooms* (1963) and *Iliad of Broken Sentences* (1967).

JOHN (HOYER) UPDIKE (1932–)
American novelist, short-story writer and poet. Born in Pennsylvania. He won the Pulitzer Prize twice – for *Rabbit is Rich* (1981) and *Rabbit at Rest* (1990). His volumes of poetry include *Telephone Poles and other Poems* (1963).

TOM (RICHARD) VAUGHAN (PHILLIPS) (1950–)
Tom Phillips entered the foreign and commonwealth office in 1983. In 2000 he was appointed British High Commissioner to Uganda. He is married with two children.

ALICE (MALSENIOR) WALKER (1944–)
Poet and novelist. Born in Eatonton, Georgia, Walker wrote *The Color Purple*, for which she won a Pulitzer Prize in 1983. Among her books of poetry are *Once* (1968) and *Horses Make a Landscape Look More Beautiful* (1984).

ANNA WICKHAM (EDITH ALICE MARY HARPER) (1884–1947)
Born in Wimbledon and educated in Australia before training as an opera singer in Paris. Her work includes *The Contemplative Quarry* (1915), *The Little Old House* (1921) and *Thirty-Six New Poems* (1936).

C. K. WILLIAMS (1936–)
American poet. C. K. Williams was born in New Jersey. He currently teaches creative writing at Princeton and divides his time between Paris and America. His collection *Repair* won the Pulitzer Prize for Poetry in 2000.

HUGO WILLIAMS (1942–)
British poet. Born in Windsor, the son of actor Hugh Williams, he published his first volume of poetry

in 1965, *Symptoms of Loss*. His latest work includes *Dock Leaves* (1994) and *Billy's Rain* (1999).

WILLIAM WORDSWORTH (1770–1850)
British poet. Born in Cockermouth, Cumberland. In 1843 he succeeded his friend Robert Southey to the office of Poet Laureate. His work includes *Poems, in Two Volumes* (1807) and *Lyrical Ballads* (1798), whose second edition featured a preface that became a manifesto of the Romantic movement.

W.B. (WILLIAM BUTLER) YEATS
(1865–1939)
Irish poet and playwright. Born in Dublin, Yeats had a lifelong interest in mysticism and the occult. He was also one of the founders of the Abbey Theatre in Dublin. Yeats was awarded the Nobel Prize in 1923. His most famous poems include 'No Second Troy', 'The Lake Isle of Innisfree', 'He wishes for the cloths of heaven', 'When you are old' and 'Easter, 1916'.

ACKNOWLEDGEMENTS

Fleur Adcock: 'Happy Ending', copyright © Fleur Adcock, from *Poems 1960–2000* (Bloodaxe Books, 2000), reprinted by permission of the publisher. **Maya Angelou**: 'The Lie', 'The Telephone', 'Where We Belong: A Duet', and 'Changing' from *Complete Collected Poems* (Virago Press, 1994), reprinted by permission of Time Warner Books UK and Random House, Inc. **Margaret Atwood**: 'Siren Song' from *Selected Poems 1965–1975* (Virago Press, 1975), reprinted by permission of Time Warner Books UK and Curtis Brown Ltd. **W. H. Auden**: 'Twelve Songs IX' ('Funeral Blues'), 'Alone' and 'The More Loving One' from *The Collected Poems* (1976), copyright 1940 and renewed 1968 by W. H. Auden, reprinted by permission of the publishers, Faber & Faber Ltd and Random House, Inc. **Connie Beasley**: 'Permissive Society' from *Central Reservations: New and Selected Poems* (Bloodaxe Books, 1990), reprinted by permission of the publisher. **John Betjeman**: 'In a Bath Teashop' from *Collected Poems* (John Murray, 1978), reprinted by permission of John Murray (Publishers) Ltd. **Earle Birney**: 'From the Hazel Bough' from *The Bear on the Delhi Road* (Chatto & Windus, 1973), reprinted by permission of the Executor of the Estate of Earle Birney. **Elizabeth Bishop**: 'One Art' from *The Complete Poems: 1927–1979*, copyright © 1979, 1983 by Alice Helen Methfessel, reprinted by permission of Farrar, Straus & Giroux, LLC; 'It is Marvellous to Wake Up Together', uncollected poem published in Lorrie Goldensohn: *Elizabeth Bishop: The Biography of a Poetry* (Columbia University Press, 1992). **Nina Bourne**: 'Where the SIngle Men Go in Summer' first published in *The New Yorker*, 14 July 1951, reprinted by permission of the author and The Condé Nast Publications. **Eleanor Brown**: 'Bitcherel' from *Maiden Speech* (Bloodaxe Books, 1996), reprinted by permission of the publisher. **Charles Bukowski**: 'wearing the collar' from *You Get So Alone at Times That It Just Makes Sense* (Black Sparrow Press, 1986), copyright © Charles Bukowski 1986, reprinted by permission of HarperCollins*Publishers*. **Alistair Te Ariki Campbell**: 'To Rid Myself of You' from *Collected Poems 1947–1981* (Alister Taylor, 1981). **Raymond Carver**: 'Late Fragment' from *All Of Us: The Collected Poems* (first published in Great Britain by Harvill, 1996), © Tess Gallagher 1996, reprinted by permission of The Random House Group Ltd and International Creative Management, Inc. **C. P. Cavafy**: 'Valedictory' (from 'Ithaka') from *C. P. Cavafy: The Collected Poems* translated by Edmund Keeley and Philip Sherrard, edited by George Savidis (The Hogarth Press, 1984), translation copyright © Edmund Keeley and Philip Sherrard 1975, 1984, reprinted by permission of The Random House Group Ltd on behalf of the Estate of C. P. Cavafy, and Rogers, Coleridge & White Ltd, 20 Powis Mews, London W11 1JN. **John Clare**: 'First Love' from Eric Robinson and David Powell (eds.): *John Clare: The Oxford Authors* (OUP, 1984), © Eric Robinson 1984, reprinted by permission of The Curtis Brown Group Ltd, London, on behalf of Eric Robinson. **Mandy Coe**: 'Go to Bed with a Cheese & Pickle Sandwich' first published in *Eating Your Cake and Having It* edited by Ann Gray (Fatchance Press, 1997), reprinted by permission of the author. **Wendy Cope**: 'Bloody Men',

'Defining the Problem', 'Two Cures for Love', and 'Loss' from *Serious Concerns* (1992); 'Giving Up Smoking' from *Making Cocoa for Kingsley Amis* (1986), reprinted by permission of the publisher, Faber & Faber Ltd. **E. E. Cummings**: 'may i feel said he' and 'it may not always be so;and i say' from *Complete Poems 1904–1962* edited by George J. Firmage, copyright © 1991 by the Trustees for the E. E. Cummings Trust and George James Firmage, reprinted by permission of the publishers, W. W. Norton & Company. **Cecil Day-Lewis**: 'Walking Away' from *Collected Poems* (Cape, 1954/reissued by The Estate, 1998), reprinted by permission of PFD on behalf of the author. **Emily Dickinson**: 'They Might Not Need Me', 'Wild Nights', and 'After Great Pain, A Formal Feeling Comes' from *The Poems of Emily Dickinson* edited by Ralph W. Franklin (The Belknap Press of Harvard University Press, Cambridge, Mass), copyright © 1998 by the President and Fellows of Harvard College, copyright © 1951, 1955, 1979 by the President and Fellows of Harvard College, reprinted by permission of the publishers and the Trustees of Amherst College. **Moyra Donaldson**: 'Infidelities' from *Snakeskin Stilettos* (CavanKerry Press Ltd, 2002), reprinted by permission of the author and the publisher. **Carol Ann Duffy**: 'The *Darling* Letters' from *The Other Country* (Anvil Press Poetry, 1990), reprinted by permission of the publisher. **Gavin Ewart**: 'Ending' from *The Collected Ewart 1933–1980* (Hutchinson, 1980), reprinted by permission of Margo Ewart. **Vicki Feaver**: 'Coat' and 'Love Poem' from *Close Relatives* (Secker & Warburg, 1981), reprinted by permission of the author. **James Fenton**: 'Let's Go Over it Again' first published in *The New Yorker*, 14 May 2001, copyright © James Fenton 2001, reprinted by permission of PFD on behalf of the author. **Robert Frost**: 'Acquainted with the Night' from *The Poetry of Robert Frost* edited by Edward Connery Lathem (Henry Holt & Company/Jonathan Cape), copyright © 1936, 1951 by Robert Frost, copyright 1964 by Lesley Frost Ballantine, copyright 1923, 1969 by Henry Holt & Company, LLC, reprinted by permission of the Estate of Robert Frost and the publishers, The Random House Group Ltd and Henry Holt & Company, LLC. **Pamela Gillilan**: 'Home is the Hunter' from *All-Steel Traveller* (Bloodaxe Books, 1994), reprinted by permission of the publisher. **Robert Graves**: 'Symptoms of Love' from *Complete Poems* (1997), reprinted by permission of the publisher, Carcanet Press Ltd. **Sophie Hannah**: 'The End of Love' from *Hero and the Girl Next Door* (1995), reprinted by permission of the publisher, Carcanet Press Ltd. **Seamus Heaney**: 'The Skunk' from *Opened Ground: Poems 1966–1996* (1998), copyright © Seamus Heaney 1998, reprinted by permission of the publishers, Faber & Faber Ltd and Farrar, Straus & Giroux, LLC. **Heinrich Heine**: 'They Loved Each Other' ('Es Stehen Unbeweglich') translated by Aaron Kramer from *The Poetry and Prose of Heinrich Heine* (Citadel Press, 1969), copyright © 1969 by Citadel Press, Inc, reprinted by permission of Citadel Press/Kensington Publishing Corporation. www.kensingtonbooks.com. All rights reserved. **Helene Johnson**: 'Futility' from *This Waiting for Love* (University of Massachusetts Press, 2001), reprinted by permission of the publisher. **Erica Jong**: 'The Cabala According to Thomas Alva Edison' from *Fruits and Vegetables* (Secker & Warburg 1973). **Philip Larkin**: 'Talking in Bed' from *Collected Poems* (1990), copyright © The Estate of Philip Larkin 1988, 1989 reprinted by permission of the publishers, Faber & Faber Ltd and Farrar, Straus & Giroux, LLC. **C. S. Lewis**: 'Joys that Sting' from *Poems* (Faber, 1964), copyright © C. S. Lewis Pte. Ltd. 1964, reprinted by permission of the C. S. Lewis Company and Harcourt, Inc. **Liz Lochhead**: 'I Wouldn't Thank You for a Valentine' from *True Confessions and New Cliches* (Polygon, 1985), reprinted by permission of Edinburgh University Press. **Roger McGough**:

Collections, Wellesley College Library. **A. S. J. Tessimond**: 'Two Men in a Dance Hall', 'Acknowledgement' and 'The Same Hour Will Not Strike' from *Collected Poems of A. S. J. Tessimond* edited by Hubert Nicholson (White Knights Press, 1985), reprinted by permission of Sadie Williams. **R. S. Thomas**: 'A Marriage' from *Mass for Hard Times* (Bloodaxe Books, 1992), reprinted by permission of the publisher. **Rosemary Tonks**: 'Story of a Hotel Room' from *Notes on Cafes and Bedrooms* (Putnam, 1963), copyright © Rosemary Tonks 1975, reprinted by permission of Sheil Land Associates. **John Updike**: 'All the While' from *Collected Poems 1953–1993* (Knopf/Hamish Hamilton 1993, Penguin 1995), copyright © John Updike 1993, 1995, reprinted by permission of Penguin Books Ltd and Random House, Inc. **Tom Vaughan**: 'Proposal', first published in *Orbis* 108/9, Spring/Summer 1998, reprinted by permission of the author. **Alice Walker**: 'I'm Really Very Fond' from *Horses Make a Landscape Look More Beautiful* (The Women's Press, 1985), copyright © 1979 by Alice Walker, reprinted by permission of David Higham Associates and Harcourt, Inc. **Anna Wickam**: 'The Fired Pot' from *The Writings of Anna Wickham* edited by R. D. Smith (Virago Press, 1984), reprinted by permission of George Hepburn and Margaret Hepburn. **C. K. Williams**: 'Love: Beginnings' from *New and Selected Poems* (Bloodaxe Books, 1995), reprinted by permission of the publisher. **Hugo Williams**: 'Saturday Morning' from *Collected Poems* (Faber, 2002), reprinted by permission of the publisher, Faber & Faber Ltd. **W. B. Yeats**: 'He wishes for the cloths of heaven' and 'When you are old' from *The Collected Poems of W. B. Yeats*, edited by Richard J. Finneran (Macmillan, 1983), reprinted by permission of A. P. Watt on behalf of Michael B. Yeats.

Although we have tried to trace and contact all copyright holders before publication, this has not been possible in every case. If notified, the publisher will be pleased to make any necessary arrangements to rectify errors and omissions at the earliest opportunity.

INDEX